THE ANNOTATED LUTHER STUDY EDITION

Little Prayer Book

1522

and

A Simple Way to Pray

1535

THE ANNOTATED LUTHER STUDY EDITION

Little Prayer Book, 1522

and

A Simple Way to Pray, 1535

MARY JANE HAEMIG

and

ERIC LUND

Fortress Press
Minneapolis

Little Prayer Book, 1522
and *A Simple Way to Pray, 1535*
THE ANNOTATED LUTHER STUDY EDITION

Excerpted from The Annotated Luther, Volume 4, *Pastoral Writings*
(Minneapolis: Fortress Press, 2016), Mary Jane Haemig, volume editor.

Fortress Press Publication Staff:
Scott Tunseth, Project Editor
Alicia Ehlers, Production Manager
Laurie Ingram, Cover Design
Michael Moore, Permissions

Copyeditor: David Lott
Series design and typesetting: Ann Delgehausen, Trio Bookworks
Proofreader: Paul Kobelski, The HK Scriptorium

Library of Congress Cataloging-in-Publication Data is available

Print ISBN: 978-1-5064-3245-8
eISBN: 978-1-5064-3246-5

The paper used in this publication meets the minimum requirements of American National Standard for Information Sciences—Permanence of Paper for Printed Library Materials, ANSI Z329, 48-1984.

Manufactured in the U.S.A.

Contents

Publisher's Note

About the Annotated Luther Study Edition

The volumes in The Annotated Luther Study Edition series have first been published in one of the comprehensive volumes of The Annotated Luther series. A description of that series and the volumes can be found in the Series Introduction (p. vii). While each comprehensive Annotated Luther volume can easily be used in classroom settings, we also recognize that treatises are often assigned individually for reading and study. To facilitate classroom and group use, we have pulled key treatises along with their introductions, annotations, and images directly from The Annotated Luther series volumes.

Please note that the study edition page numbers match the page numbers of the larger Annotated Luther volume in which it first appeared. We have intentionally retained the same page numbering to facilitate use of the study editions and larger volumes side by side.

Little Prayer Book, 1522, and *A Simple Way to Pray, 1535*,
were first published in The Annotated Luther series,
Volume 4, *Pastoral Writings* (2016).

Series Introduction

Engaging the Essential Luther

Even after five hundred years Martin Luther continues to engage and challenge each new generation of scholars and believers alike. With 2017 marking the five-hundredth anniversary of Luther's *95 Theses*, Luther's theology and legacy are being explored around the world with new questions and methods and by diverse voices. His thought invites ongoing examination, his writings are a staple in classrooms and pulpits, and he speaks to an expanding assortment of conversation partners who use different languages and hale from different geographical and social contexts.

The six volumes of The Annotated Luther edition offer a flexible tool for the global reader of Luther, making many of his most important writings available in the *lingua franca* of our times as one way of facilitating interest in the Wittenberg reformer. They feature new introductions, annotations, revised translations, and textual notes, as well as visual enhancements (illustrations, art, photos, maps, and timelines). The Annotated Luther edition embodies Luther's own cherished principles of communication. Theological writing, like preaching, needs to reflect human beings' lived experience, benefits from up-to-date scholarship, and should be easily accessible to all. These volumes are designed to help teachers and students, pastors and laypersons, and other professionals in ministry understand the context in which the documents were written, recognize how the documents have shaped Protestant and Lutheran thinking, and interpret the meaning of these documents for faith and life today.

The Rationale for This Edition

For any reader of Luther, the sheer number of his works presents a challenge. Well over one hundred volumes comprise the scholarly edition of Luther's works, the so-called Weimar Ausgabe (WA), a publishing enterprise begun in 1883 and only completed in the twenty-first century. From 1955 to 1986, fifty-five volumes came to make up *Luther's Works* (American Edition) (LW), to which Concordia Publishing House, St. Louis, is adding still more. This English-language contribution to Luther studies, matched by similar translation projects for Erasmus of Rotterdam and John Calvin, provides a theological and historical gold mine for those interested in studying Luther's thought. But even these volumes are not always easy to use and are hardly portable. Electronic forms have increased availability, but preserving Luther in book form and providing readers with manageable selections are also important goals.

Moreover, since the publication of the WA and the first fifty-five volumes of the LW, research on the Reformation in general and on Martin Luther in particular has broken new ground and evolved, as has knowledge regarding the languages in which Luther wrote. Up-to-date information from a variety of sources is brought together in The Annotated Luther, building on the work done by previous generations of scholars. The language and phrasing of the translations have also been updated to reflect modern English usage. While the WA and, in a derivative way, LW remain the central source for Luther scholarship, the present critical and annotated English translation facilitates research internationally and invites a new generation of readers for whom Latin and German might prove an unsurpassable obstacle to accessing Luther. The WA provides the basic Luther texts (with some exceptions); the LW provides the basis for almost all translations.

Defining the "Essential Luther"

Deciding which works to include in this collection was not easy. Criteria included giving attention to Luther's initial key works; considering which publications had the most impact in his day and later; and taking account of Luther's own favorites, texts addressing specific issues of continued importance for today, and Luther's exegetical works. Taken as a whole, these works present the many sides of Luther, as reformer, pastor, biblical interpreter, and theologian. To serve today's readers and by using categories similar to those found in volumes 31–47 of Luther's works (published by Fortress Press), the volumes offer in the main a thematic rather than strictly chronological approach to Luther's writings. The volumes in the series include:

> Volume 1: *The Roots of Reform* (Timothy J. Wengert, editor)
> Volume 2: *Word and Faith* (Kirsi I. Stjerna, editor)
> Volume 3: *Church and Sacraments* (Paul W. Robinson, editor)
> Volume 4: *Pastoral Writings* (Mary Jane Haemig, editor)
> Volume 5: *Christian Life in the World* (Hans J. Hillerbrand, editor)
> Volume 6: *The Interpretation of Scripture* (Euan K. Cameron, editor)

The History of the Project

In 2011 Fortress Press convened an advisory board to explore the promise and parameters of a new English edition of Luther's essential works. Board members Denis Janz, Robert Kolb, Peter Matheson, Christine Helmer, and Kirsi Stjerna deliberated with

Fortress Press publisher Will Bergkamp to develop a concept and identify contributors. After a review with scholars in the field, college and seminary professors, and pastors, it was concluded that a single-language edition was more desirable than dual-language volumes.

In August 2012, Hans Hillerbrand, Kirsi Stjerna, and Timothy Wengert were appointed as general editors of the series with Scott Tunseth from Fortress Press as the project editor. The general editors were tasked with determining the contents of the volumes and developing the working principles of the series. They also helped with the identification and recruitment of additional volume editors, who in turn worked with the general editors to identify volume contributors. Mastery of the languages and unique knowledge of the subject matter were key factors in identifying contributors. Most contributors are North American scholars and native English speakers, but The Annotated Luther includes among its contributors a circle of international scholars. Likewise, the series is offered for a global network of teachers and students in seminary, university, and college classes, as well as pastors, lay teachers, and adult students in congregations seeking background and depth in Lutheran theology, biblical interpretation, and Reformation history.

Editorial Principles

The volume editors and contributors have, with few exceptions, used the translations of LW as the basis of their work, retranslating from the WA for the sake of clarity and contemporary usage. Where the LW translations have been substantively altered, explanatory notes have often been provided. More importantly, contributors have provided marginal notes to help readers understand theological and historical references. Introductions have been expanded and sharpened to reflect the very latest historical and theological research. In citing the Bible, care has been taken to reflect the German and Latin texts commonly used in the sixteenth century rather than modern editions, which often employ textual sources that were unavailable to Luther and his contemporaries.

Finally, all pieces in The Annotated Luther have been revised in the light of modern principles of inclusive language. This is not always an easy task with a historical author, but an intentional effort has been made to revise language throughout, with creativity and editorial liberties, to allow Luther's theology to speak free from unnecessary and unintended gender-exclusive language. This important principle provides an opportunity to translate accurately certain gender-neutral German and Latin expressions that Luther employed—for example, the Latin word *homo* and the German *Mensch* mean "human being," not simply "males." Using the words *man* and *men* to translate such terms would create an ambiguity not present in the original texts. The focus is on linguistic accuracy and Luther's intent. Regarding creedal formulations and trinitarian language, Luther's own expressions have been preserved, without entering the complex and important contemporary debates over language for God and the Trinity.

The 2017 anniversary of the publication of the *95 Theses* is providing an opportunity to assess the substance of Luther's role and influence in the Protestant Reformation. Revisiting Luther's essential writings not only allows reassessment of Luther's rationale and goals but also provides a new look at what Martin Luther was about and why new generations would still wish to engage him. We hope these six volumes offer a compelling invitation.

Hans J. Hillerbrand
Kirsi I. Stjerna
Timothy J. Wengert
General Editors

Abbreviations

AWA	Archiv für die Weimarer Ausgabe
BC	*The Book of Concord*, ed. Robert Kolb and Timothy J. Wengert (Minneapolis: Fortress Press, 2000)
Brecht	Martin Brecht, *Martin Luther*, trans. James L. Schaaf, 3 vols. (Philadelphia and Minneapolis: Fortress Press, 1985–1993)
CA	Augsburg Confession
CSEL	*Corpus scriptorum ecclesiasticorum latinorum*
LC	*The Large Catechism*
LW	*Luther's Works* [American edition], ed. Helmut Lehmann and Jaroslav Pelikan, 55 vols. (Philadelphia: Fortress Press; St. Louis: Concordia, 1955–86)
MLStA	*Martin Luther: Studienausgabe*, ed. Hans-Ulrich Delius, 6 vols. (Berlin and Leipzig: Evangelische Verlagsanstalt, 1979–99)
MPG	*Patrologiae cursus completus, series Graeca*, ed. Jacques-Paul Migne, 166 vols. (Paris, 1857–1866)
MPL	*Patrologiae cursus completus, series Latina*, ed. Jacques-Paul Migne, 217 vols. (Paris, 1844–1864)
ODCC	*The Oxford Dictionary of the Christian Church*, ed. F. L. Cross, 3rd ed. rev., ed. E. A. Livingstone (Oxford: Oxford University Press, 2005)
OER	*Oxford Encyclopedia of the Reformation*, ed. Hans J. Hillerbrand, 4 vols. (New York and Oxford: Oxford University Press, 1996)
SA	*The Smalcald Articles*
SC	*The Small Catechism*
SD	*Solid Declaration*
TAL	The Annotated Luther
VD	*Verzeichnis der im deutschen Sprachbereich erschienenen Drucke des Jahrhunderts* (Munich: Bayerische Staatsbibliothek; Herzog August Bibliothek in Wolfenbüttel, Stuttgart: Hiersemann [1983–])
WA	*Luthers Werke: Kritische Gesamtausgabe* [*Schriften*], 73 vols. (Weimar: H. Böhlau, 1883–2009)
WA Bi	*Luthers Werke: Kritische Gesamtausgabe: Bibel*, 12 vols. (Weimar: H. Böhlau, 1906–61), 7:206
WA Br	*Luthers Werke: Kritische Gesamtausgabe: Briefwechsel*, 18 vols. (Weimar: H. Böhlau, 1930–1985)
WA DB	*Luthers Werke: Kritische Gesamtausgabe: Deutsche Bibel*, 12 vols. (Weimar: H. Böhlau, 1906–61)
WA TR	*Luthers Werke: Kritische Gesamtausgabe: Tischreden*, 6 vols. (Weimar: H. Böhlau, 1912–21)

The cover of a 1529 version
of Luther's *Little Prayer Book*

Little Prayer Book

1522

MARY JANE HAEMIG

INTRODUCTION

Luther's *Betbüchlein* (*Little Prayer Book*) was first published at the end of May 1522.[a] Luther had returned to Wittenberg from the Wartburg in early March 1522. The Reformation had advanced rapidly in Wittenberg, and not always in ways that Luther found helpful and evangelical. He clearly saw the need to reform worship and devotional practices but rejected enforced measures (such as the destruction of images or compelling people to receive both kinds), and instead desired a reformation embodying evangelical freedom based on the proclaimed word and faith. His *Invocavit Sermons*[b] expressed his vision of such reform.

The events of the first half of 1522 illustrate key theological insights. Luther believed that God deals with humans first outwardly, then inwardly. The external word—the speaking of the gospel, baptism, and the Lord's Supper—precedes and causes the inward experience of the Holy Spirit and faith. God gives the inward only through the outward. Faith then produces outward

---

a Martin Brecht, *Martin Luther: Shaping and Defining the Reformation 1521–1532*, trans. James L. Schaaf (Minneapolis: Fortress Press, 1990), 119 (hereafter Brecht 2).

b See above, pp. 7–45.

1. Luther later went into great detail on his differences with Karlstadt. See *Against the Heavenly Prophets in the Matter of Images and Sacraments* (1525) (LW 40:79–223; TAL 2:39–125). For more on Karlstadt in this volume, see the introduction to the *Invocavit Sermons*, pp. 7–14.

expressions. Decisions on outward matters of Christian practice, matters neither commanded nor forbidden by God, follow in evangelical freedom from faith. Luther complained that Andreas Bodenstein von Karlstadt (1486–1541) and his followers had, in both cases, reversed the direction.[1] Luther's *Betbüchlein* can be seen as a continuation of his message in the *Invocavit Sermons* and elsewhere; it provided both another proclamation of God's word and the resources for the life of faith and its outward expressions in practice that follow from that proclamation of the word. It did not mandate certain prayers and practices but provided resources for Christians to use in exercising their faith in freedom.

Luther's efforts in these months aimed at reorienting the reforming movement to its central message. In late April and early May 1522, Luther undertook a preaching tour to other cities in Electoral Saxony.[c] He was also revising his translation of the New Testament for its publication in September. It was this flurry of activity that may have prompted his comment that he "did not have the time" for a basic and thorough reformation of prayer books. Nevertheless, this work continued Luther's efforts to reform prayer practice. Already published were his sermons on the Lord's Prayer and on Rogation prayer.[d] The *Betbüchlein* reveals how profoundly Luther's Reformation insights affected the most ordinary aspects of Christian practice.

Medieval monastic prayer practices, patterns, and materials often set the pattern or ideal for lay prayer. The daily routine of monks and nuns included set times for prayer. Prayer was systematically taught even in mendicant orders.[e] The Franciscans, for example, developed a rich literature to instruct novices and friars in proper prayer practice. While they considered vocal prayer, and particularly the Lord's Prayer, as important, they also sought to reach beyond vocal prayer to mental or spiritual prayer, viewed as more advanced because it involved the human soul rising to God and attaining insights into divine secrets. Prayer was also shaped by confessional practices. It was part of

c   Brecht 2:67.

d   See above, pp. 147–57.

e   See, e.g., Bert Roest, "The Discipline of the Heart: Pedagogies of Prayer in Medieval Franciscan Works of Religious Instruction," in Timothy J. Johnson, ed., *Franciscans at Prayer* (Leiden/Boston: Brill, 2007), 413–48.

the "satisfaction" stage in penance, in that saying prayers after proper contrition and confession to a priest helped satisfy the penitent's remaining temporal penalty for sin. Pastoral and devotional materials made clear that prayer was an activity that gained merit for the one praying, but that such merit depended on the fulfillment of the proper conditions.[2]

In the late Middle Ages, Books of Hours also became popular,[f] many being designed for and used by laity. Some are known to us today as finely bound and richly illuminated books used by nobility. With the invention of printing in the mid-fifteenth century, such books were available to a broader audience. These books centered on a cycle of prayers to the Virgin Mary (the Hours of the Virgin), designed for recitation throughout the day. The books offered materials and patterns that paralleled monastic practices but were aimed at a lay audience. Commonly, such books included calendars with feast days and commemorations of saints, Gospel lessons touching on major events in the life of Christ and often supplemented by John's account of Christ's passion, the Hours of the Virgin (eight separate hours including psalms, hymns, prayers, and lessons), the Hours of the Cross, the Hours of the Holy Spirit, specialized prayers to the Virgin, the seven penitential psalms (6, 32, 38, 51, 102, 130, and 143), the office of the dead, and prayers to the saints. The books

2. As Guido of Monte Rochen wrote in a popular pastoral manual in his discussion of the Sacrament of Penance: "For prayer to be entirely meritorious and effective as satisfaction, it is required to have thirteen conditions, namely, that it be faithful, untroubled,

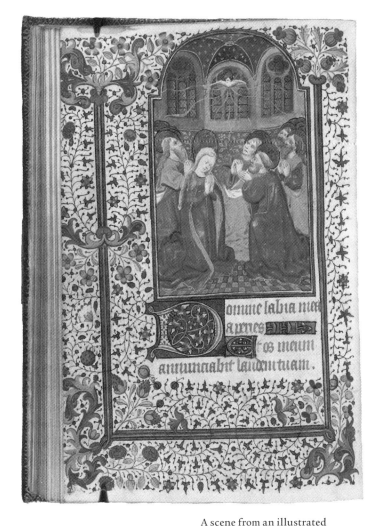

A scene from an illustrated Book of Hours printed in the fifteenth century depicts prayer and the Holy Spirit as dove.

f   Roger S. Wieck, "Prayer for the People: The Book of Hours," in Roy Hammerling, ed., *A History of Prayer: The First to the Fifteenth Century* (Leiden: Brill, 2008), 388–416.

humble, discrete, shameful, devout, secret, pure, tearful, attentive, fervent, painstaking, and constant." Guido of Monte Rochen, *Handbook for Curates: A Late Medieval Manual on Pastoral Ministry*, trans. Anne T. Thayer, with an introduction by Anne T. Thayer and Katharine J. Lualdi (Washington, DC: Catholic University of America Press, 2011), 247.

The *Stabat Mater*. Mary, the mother of Jesus, stands by Christ's cross along with the apostle John. Painting by Roger van der Weyden (1399/1400–1464).

also exhibited a wide variation in other content. Some contained Masses, that is, the prayers said by the priest or sung by the choir; some contained a variety of other prayers, including the *Stabat Mater* and prayers to one's guardian angel. Some prayers were accompanied by indulgences that provided the user with extra merit.

In Germany, beginning at the end of the fifteenth century, the most popular and widely disseminated prayer books were known as the *Hortulus animae* ("Garden of the Soul" or "Garden of the Spirit"). While including the typical contents of the Books of Hours, these shifted the focus of prayer away from the monastic routine and toward the personal and devotional use of prayer. They included prayers for arising and going to bed, prayers for leaving the house and for entering the church, prayers (often from the church fathers) to gain indulgences, prayers while receiving the sacraments of penance and the Lord's Supper, and prayers while attending Mass.[g]

Other extant works offer insight into the practice of prayer in the late medieval period. One prayer book for laity, probably dating from the late fifteenth or early sixteenth century, contained a hymn of praise to Mary, three prayers to one's personal angel, two prayers to an apostle chosen to be one's patron saint, and three prayers to Saint Erasmus.[h]

The lines between catechism, prayer book, and breviary were not strictly drawn in the Middle Ages, nor were lines between materials meant for communal worship and those meant for private devotion. The Ten Commandments, Apostles' Creed, Lord's Prayer, and Hail Mary (*Ave Maria*) were common elements of medieval catechisms. Typically, these catechisms also con-

[g]   Traugott Koch discusses the *Hortulus animae* in *Johann Habermanns "Betbüchlein" im Zusammenhang seiner Theologie* (Tübingen: Mohr Siebeck, 2001), 12–13. For more on these prayer books, see Austra Reinis, *Reforming the Art of Dying: The* Ars Moriendi *in the German Reformation (1519–1528)* (Burlington, VT: Ashgate, 2007), 40–45.

[h]   Peter Matheson, "Angels, Depression, and 'The Stone': A Late Medieval Prayer Book," *Journal of Theological Studies* (NS) 48, no. 2 (October 1997): 517–30.

tained other materials designed to guide conduct, educate the Christian in the faith, and teach prayer.[i] As most people were illiterate, they would have learned their prayers by hearing them spoken and repeating them.

Luther sought to reform both the theology and practice of prayer. He realized that unless his insights were conveyed on a popular, understandable level, they would not succeed in changing longstanding, strongly rooted ideas and practice. Medieval prayer books and practices had left people with many ideas that undermined God's mercy received in faith. Luther sought to encourage simple direct prayer to God, who had promised to hear the one praying, rather than to the Virgin Mary and the saints. Luther stressed that God hears prayers, despite unworthiness, because God has promised to listen to prayer. Prayer is not a good work and does not earn indulgences[3] or anything else from God; it is honest communication with God. Mindless repetition of prayer is not helpful; instead, Christians should contemplate the meaning of each petition and boldly, honestly, and persistently present their needs to God.

This illustration from a *Hortulus animae* published in 1550 depicts the branch springing from the stump of Jesse (Isaiah 11). As Jesse, the father of David, lies on the ground a tree grows from his side at whose center is the Madonna and child.

The *Betbüchlein* gave laypeople an evangelical counterpart to the problematic prayer books that Luther saw in use. In its effort to shape lay piety by focusing on the Ten Commandments, Apostles' Creed, and Lord's Prayer, the work is decidedly catechetical and reflects what would later become the structure of his catechisms.[4] Luther thought that the best way to teach prayer was to introduce people to the faith and thereby to incite them

3. Indulgences purported to remit a certain number of years that the Christian had to serve in purgatory.

4. See Luther's reflections in the *Prayer Book*'s introduction (below). See also his comment in the preface to the *Deutsche Messe* (German Mass), 1525 (LW 53:64–66; TAL 3:142–46), where he emphasizes the need for a catechism and suggests using the *Betbüchlein* as a basis for evangelical catechisms.

i   See for example, Dietrich Kolde's "Mirror for Christians" (1480), in Denis Janz, *Three Reformation Catechisms: Catholic, Anabaptist, Lutheran* (Lewiston, NY: Edwin Mellen Press, 1982), 29–130 (hereafter Kolde).

5. Commenting on Strassburg, Miriam Usher Chrisman writes, "The most popular prayerbook, of which five editions were printed between 1560 and 1591, was Luther's own *Betbüchlein.*" Miriam Usher Chrisman, *Lay Culture, Learned Culture: Books and Social Change in Strasbourg, 1580–1599* (New Haven: Yale University Press, 1982), 88.

6. See Luther's preface to Casper Cruciger's *Summer Postil* (1544) (LW 77:9; WA 21:201): "So also the shameful, false, slanderous prayer books, of which the world was full, have been cleared out, and in place of them pure prayers and good Christian hymns have been published, especially the Psalter, the finest and most precious prayer book and hymnal of them all, concerning which no theologian of our time could boast that he had understood a single psalm as well and as thoroughly as the laypeople, men and women, understand them now."

7. The title *"Betbüchlein"* literally means "Little Prayer Book." The "*-lein*" is a diminutive in German. This translation is based on the German text in WA 10/2:375–501 and the translation by Martin H. Bertram in LW 43:11–45.

to prayer. Here, as in other places, he focused his discussion of prayers on the Lord's Prayer. As he did frequently in later works, he also advocated the use of biblical texts, here the Psalms, as prayer for Christians. Luther and his followers saw clearly that in order to shape faith and practice, accessible materials had to make his insights available and usable at the popular level.

It is striking that this work is not a collection of prayers. For this reason, one scholar has called it an "anti-prayer book."[j] It actually is not a "prayer book" as that literary genre had been understood, for it contains no written prayers (such as the morning, evening, and table prayers that his *Small Catechism* later included) but, rather, direction and advice concerning prayer. Luther encouraged the use of biblical texts—particularly the Lord's Prayer and the Psalms—as something the Christian could use to pray meditatively and in so doing bring his or her own situation before God.[k] Luther's prayer book exhibits both Luther's reforming insights and his pastoral insights into how to convey them. He used familiar elements, common in medieval prayer books but now understood in an evangelical way, to convey Reformation content. The absence of other elements indicated that they did not fit his theology.

The work has a complicated publication history, as Luther himself—and those after him—modified its contents. Ironically, the same thing happened to it that happened to many medieval prayer books: while the basic core (Ten Commandments, Creed, Lord's Prayer, and Hail Mary) remained intact, various elements were added to and subtracted from it. Luther sometimes included translations of various books of the New Testament, psalms, and relevant sermons. Subsequent editors of the work also added various elements—for example, forms for use in confessing sin, instruction for the dying, short explanations of the Lord's Prayer, and the like. One of the more thorough revisions, probably done under Luther's supervision, took place in 1529, when the printer added a set of fifty woodcuts depicting the basic story of salvation from the creation, through the fall,

j   Johannes Wallmann, "Zwischen Herzensgebet und Gebetbuch. Zur protestantischen deutschen Gebetsliteratur im 17. Jahrhundert," in *Gebetsliteratur der frühen Neuzeit als Hausfrömmigkeit* (Wiesbaden: Harrassowitz, 2001), 19.

k   See the discussion in ibid., 18–21.

the incarnation, death, resurrection, and ascension of Christ, to the second coming, ending with the spreading of the gospel throughout the world.

Luther's *Betbüchlein* became popular immediately. It was printed at least seventeen times between 1522 and 1525 (in Augsburg, Erfurt, Grimma, Wittenberg, Jena, and Strassburg) and at least forty-four times by the end of the century.[1] In some areas, it was the most popular prayer book.[5] Writing in 1544, Luther claimed success for all evangelical efforts, including his own, to reform prayer practice.[6]

LITTLE PRAYER BOOK[7]

TO ALL MY DEAR MASTERS and brothers[8] in Christ, grace and peace.

Among the many harmful books and doctrines by which Christians are misled and deceived and countless false beliefs have arisen, I regard the little prayer books as by no means the least objectionable. They drub into the minds of simple people such a wretched counting up of sins[9] and going to confession, such un-Christian foolishness about prayers to God and the saints! Moreover, these books are puffed up with promises of indulgences[10] and come out with decorations in red ink and pretty titles; one is called *Hortulus animae*, another *Paradisus animae*,[11] and so on. These books need a basic and thorough reformation if not total extermination. And I would make the same judgment about those passionals[12] or books of legends into which the devil has tossed his own additions. But I just don't have the time and it is too much for me to undertake such a reformation alone. So until God gives me more time and grace, I

8. Luther prefaced his new prayer book with a letter of explanation addressed to "*herrn*" and "*brudern*." *Herrn* ("sirs") could refer to *Pfarrherrn* (parish pastors) or to *Ratsherrn* (civil officials) while *brudern* could refer to monks or others in ecclesiastical positions. Their opinions about Luther's bold supplanting of the old traditional prayer books would be solicited by many people. The support of these authorities for the new book and their recommendation would help greatly Luther's effort at reforming the forms of personal piety among the laity.

9. Numbering types of sins was common in late medieval Europe. So, for example, the seven deadly sins, the nine alien sins, the six sins against the Holy Spirit, and the five commandments of the church were all discussed in Kolde's catechism and other devotional works.

10. In medieval Roman Catholicism, certain prayers were thought to earn indulgences, that is, remission or reduction of the time one was obligated to spend in purgatory because of one's sins.

11. *Hortulus animae* ("Garden of the Soul" or "Garden of the Spirit") and *Paradisus animae* ("Paradise of the Soul") were titles for popular late medieval prayer books.

12. Passionals were histories of Christ's passion, often an amalgam of the scriptural accounts. Often other things were added to these works as well, for example, other Bible stories, stories concerning Mary, and stories concerning saints. Medieval prayer books sometimes contained one or more of these.

1 VD16, L4081–L4125.

13. The "mirror" was a literary genre. Many different types of "mirrors" were written in the late medieval to early modern era. Typically, a mirror declared what was acceptable and unacceptable conduct in a particular profession or situation. As the word *mirror* indicates, they were meant for self-examination and improvement.

14. The Lord's Prayer was commonly included in medieval catechisms and prayer books. Luther sees it as the preeminent prayer, not simply one among many.

15. Luther here implicitly rejects the imposition of monastic prayer practices on the laity. Such attempts manifested themselves, for example, in attempts to encourage laypeople to pray in accordance with the canonical hours. See Kolde's catechism, 88–90, where laypersons are given a prayer for each canonical hour.

16. St. Bridget (1303–1373) was a Swedish saint and mystic who was canonized in 1391. Her literary works include four prayers, but in the flowering of legends around her captivating personality, a set of fifteen prayers was ascribed to her and used frequently in the spiritual exercises of the devout. Personal prayer books promised that the Bridget prayers would gain for the user the salvation of forty souls of the same sex as the person offering the prayers, the conversion of forty sinners, and the strengthening of forty-six righteous persons.

will limit myself to the exhortation in this book. To begin with, I offer this simple Christian form of prayer and mirror[13] for recognizing sin, based on the Lord's Prayer and the Ten Commandments. And I am convinced that when Christians[m] rightly pray the Lord's Prayer[14] at any time or use any portion of it as they may desire, their praying is more than adequate.[15] What is important for a good prayer is not many words, as Christ says in Matthew 6[:7], but rather a turning to God frequently and with heartfelt longing, and doing so without ceasing [1 Thess. 5:17].

Birgitta (St. Bridget) of Sweden on an altarpiece in Salem church, Södermanland, Sweden

And herewith I urge everyone to break away from using the Bridget prayers[16] and any others that are ornamented with indulgences or rewards and urge all to get accustomed to praying this plain, ordinary Christian prayer. The longer one devotes one's self to this kind of praying, the more sweet and joyous it becomes. To that end may this prayer's Master, our dear Lord Jesus Christ, help us, to whom be blessings in all eternity. Amen.

m   This term and corresponding pronouns are masculine singular in the German.

Foreword

It was not unintended in God's particular ordering of things that a lowly Christian person who might be unable to read the Bible[17] should nevertheless be obligated to learn and know the Ten Commandments, the Creed, and the Lord's Prayer.[18] Indeed, the total content of Scripture and preaching and everything a Christian needs to know is quite fully and richly comprehended in these three items. They summarize everything with such brevity and clarity[19] that no one can complain or make any excuse that the things necessary for salvation are too complicated or difficult to remember.

Three things people must know in order to be saved. [20] First, they" must know what to do and what to leave undone. Second, when they realize that, by their own strength, they cannot measure up to what they should do or leave undone, they need to know where to seek, find, and take the strength they require. Third, they must know how to seek and obtain that strength. It is just like sick people who first have to determine the nature of their sickness, and what to do or to leave undone. After that they have to know where to get the medicine which will help them do or leave undone what is right for a healthy person. Third, they have to desire to search for this medicine and to obtain it or have it brought to them.

Thus the commandments teach humans to recognize their sickness, enabling them to see and perceive what to do or refrain from doing, consent to or refuse, and so recognize themselves to be sinful and wicked persons.[21] The Creed will teach and show them where to find the medicine—grace—which will help them to become devout and keep the commandments. The Creed points them to God and God's mercy, given and made plain in Christ. Third, the Lord's Prayer teaches how they may seek, get, and bring to themselves all this, namely, by proper, humble, consolatory prayer. So it will be given to them, and through the fulfillment of God's commandments they will be blessed. In these three are the essentials of the entire Bible.

17. Literacy rates were low, estimated at 3 to 4 percent of Germany's population, about 400,000 people. Steven Ozment, *The Age of Reform 1250-1550: An Intellectual and Religious History of Late Medieval and Reformation Europe* (New Haven: Yale University Press, 1980), 201. Also, although vernacular Bibles were available, some had no access to them.

18. In the Middle Ages, people were expected to memorize the Hail Mary, the Ten Commandments, the Apostles' Creed, and the Lord's Prayer. Luther views only the last three as necessary but does not neglect the Hail Mary.

19. Luther implicitly contrasts the simplicity of these three elements to the many elements found in medieval prayer books and catechisms.

20. In medieval catechisms, the Apostles' Creed was often placed before the Lord's Prayer and the Ten Commandments. See, for example, Kolde. Luther here explains why he has a different order of parts.

21. The Ten Commandments were used as a confessional aid in the late medieval era. The priest could, by going through the commandments, lead the penitent to recognize and confess sin. The commandments were also used as instruments and guidelines for use in forming one's faith (intellectual knowledge of Christianity) into a life pleasing to God.

n Here and following the plural pronoun replaces the singular male pronoun in the original.

22. Luther emphasized human inability to fulfill the commandments, rather than human ability to please God through them.

For this reason, we begin with the commandments,*o* to teach and perceive our sin and wickedness, that is, our spiritual sickness that prevents us from doing or leaving undone as we ought.[22]

Image of Moses receiving the Ten Commandments, from a seventeenth century reprint of Luther's Bible

The First Tablet

23. Luther often used the distinction between the first and second tables (or tablets) of the law, between the obligations humans owe to God and those humans owe to other humans.

24. Though the masculine pronoun is used here and in the following paragraphs, Luther intended that this apply to all people.

Properly, the first or right-hand tablet[23] of the commandments includes the first three, in which a person is instructed concerning his duty toward God—what he should do or leave undone, that is, how he should conduct himself in relation to God.

The First Commandment teaches a person the right attitude in his[24] own heart toward God, that is, what he should always keep in mind and consider important. In particular a person should expect all good things from God as from a father or good friend in all trust, faith, and love, with fear at all times, so he should not offend God, just as a child avoids offending his father. For Nature teaches us that there is a God who grants every good thing and who helps in all difficulties, as even the

o   Luther went into greater detail as to what each commandment requires in his *Treatise on Good Works* (1520) (LW 44:21–114; TAL 1:257–368).

false gods of the heathen declare. So the First Commandment says: "You shall have no other gods."

The Second Commandment[25] teaches how a person should govern himself in relation to God both in his outward speech to others and also in his inward, personal attitude. That is, he should honor God's name. For no one can express God's divine nature, either to himself or to others, except by using God's name. Thus this commandment says: "You shall not take the name of your God in vain."

The Third Commandment teaches how a person should govern his actions toward God, that is, in service to God.[26] It says: "You shall sanctify the Sabbath."[27] In this way these three commandments teach a person how to govern himself toward God in thought, word, and deed, that is, in all of life.

The Second Tablet

The second or left-hand tablet of the commandments includes the following seven commandments, in which a person is taught his obligation toward his fellow humans and neighbors, what he should do and leave undone.

The first teaches how to conduct one's self toward everyone in authority—those who act in God's place [Rom. 13:1-6; Eph. 6:5-8]. Hence this commandment comes immediately after the first three that relate to God's person, and it deals with those who are like God—father and mother, master and mistress. It says: "You shall honor your father and your mother."

The next commandment teaches how to deal with the person of our neighbor and fellow humans, that we are not to harm these, but help and assist them wherever they need it. It says: "You shall not kill."

The third teaches a person how to act in relation to what, next to his person, is the neighbor's most valuable possession—his wife, or child, or friend. We must not bring them into disgrace but preserve their reputation as much as we can. The commandment says: "You shall not commit adultery."

The fourth teaches a person how to act with regard to his neighbor's worldly property. One should not steal it or hinder it, but help him prosper. It says: "You shall not steal."

The fifth teaches a person how to act toward his neighbor's worldly reputation and honor. One should not weaken it but

25. Luther continues in the medieval tradition in that he does not consider the commandment against "graven images" to be the Second Commandment. See Albrecht Peters, *Commentary on Luther's Catechisms: Ten Commandments*, trans. Holger Sonntag (St. Louis: Concordia, 2009), pp. 141–46, "Appendix: The Prohibition of Images."

26. The German is *gottis diensten*, which is sometimes translated "worshiping" or "worship service," but means literally "God's service" or "service to God."

27. The German is *Feiertag heiligen. Fiertag* does not mean "day of celebration" but, rather, a day on which one rests from one's labors.

support, protect, and preserve it. It says: "You shall not give false testimony against your neighbor."

What is thus forbidden is harming one's neighbor in anything he owns; rather one should help him prosper. When we look at natural law, we see how right and universal all these commandments are. They require nothing toward God or our neighbor but that which anyone would want to see done, either from a divine or from a human point of view.

The last two commandments teach how evil our nature is and how unstained we should keep ourselves from all desires of the flesh and from greed—for us a lifelong task and struggle. These commandments read: "You shall not covet your neighbor's house. You shall not covet his wife, his servants or maids, his livestock, or anything that is his."

Christ himself summarizes the Ten Commandments briefly, saying, "Whatever you want others to do to you, do the same to them; this is the whole Law and the Prophets" [Matt. 7:12]. No one wants to see his kindness repaid by ingratitude or have someone defame his name. No one wants to be treated arrogantly, no one wants to be disobeyed, or treated with anger, or to have an unchaste wife, or to be robbed of his possessions, or endure falsehood against himself, or be betrayed, or be slandered. On the contrary, everyone wants a neighbor to show love and friendship, gratitude and helpfulness, truthfulness and loyalty—all required by these Ten Commandments.

What It Means
to Break[28] the Commandments[29]

Breaking the First

Whoever tries to do away with trouble by witchcraft, by the black arts, or by an alliance with the devil.

Whoever uses [magic] writings, signs, herbs, words, spells, and the like.[p]

28. Luther uses the term *Ubertrettung*, which means "crossing a boundary."

29. Here, as later in the *Small Catechism* (1529), Luther considers first how one breaks the commandments, and second, how one fulfills them.

p   For a discussion of popular magic and its manifestations during this era, see Robert Scribner, "The Reformation, Popular Magic, and the 'Disenchantment of the World,'" in Lyndal Roper and Rober Scribner, eds., *Religion and Culture in Germany (1400–1800)* (Leiden: Brill, 2001), 346–65.

Whoever uses divining rods, uses incantations to find trea-sure, resorts to crystal-gazing, travels by a magic cloak, or steals milk.

Whoever governs his[30] life and work according to certain days, celestial signs, and the advice of fortune-tellers [Lev. 20:6].

Whoever uses certain incantations as blessings and charms to protect himself, his cattle, his children, and any kind of prop-erty against danger from wolves, sword, fire, or water.

Whoever ascribes any bad luck or unpleasantness to the devil or to evil persons and does not, with love and praise, accept both evil and good as coming from God alone [Phil. 4:11], responding to God with gratitude and willing submission.

Whoever tempts God and exposes himself to unnecessary danger to body [Luke 4:12] and soul.

Whoever shows arrogance because of his piety, knowledge, or other spiritual gifts.

Whoever honors God and the saints only to gain some tem-poral advantage, forgetting the needs of his soul.

Whoever does not trust God at all times and rely upon God's mercy in everything he does.

Whoever doubts the Creed or God's grace.

Whoever does not defend others against unbelief and doubt and does not do all in his power to help them believe and trust in God's grace.

Here belongs every kind of unbelief, despair, and false belief.

Breaking the Second Commandment

Whoever swears needlessly or habitually.

Whoever swears a false oath or breaks his vow.

Whoever vows or swears to do evil.

Whoever curses using God's name.

Whoever tells silly stories about God and whoever carelessly misconstrues the words of Scripture.

Whoever does not call upon God's name in adversity and does not praise him in joy and sorrow, in fortune and misfor-tune [2 Cor. 6:8].

Whoever uses piety and wisdom to seek praise, honor, or rep-utation.

Whoever calls upon God's name falsely, as do heretics and all arrogant saints.

30. Though Luther uses the male pronoun here and in other places in this list of what it means to break the commandments, he means all persons.

Whoever does not praise God's name, no matter what may happen to him.

Whoever does not restrain others from dishonoring God's name, from using it wrongly or for evil purposes.

Hence self-conceit, boasting, and spiritual pride belong here.

Breaking the Third Commandment

Whoever does not listen to God's word or try to understand it.

Whoever does not pray and serve God spiritually.

Whoever does not regard all he does as God's work.

Whoever, in all he does and endures, does not quietly allow God to do with him as God pleases.

Whoever does not help the other person do all this and does not restrain him from doing otherwise.

Breaking the Fourth Commandment

Whoever is ashamed that his parents are poor, have faults, or are not highly regarded.

Whoever does not provide clothing and food for his parents in their need.

Especially whoever curses or strikes his parents, slanders them, and is hateful and disobedient toward them.

Whoever does not in all sincerity regard them highly simply because God has so commanded.

Whoever does not hold his parents in honor even though they might do wrong and use force.

Whoever does not honor those in authority over him, remain loyal and obedient to them, no matter whether they are good or bad.

Whoever does not help others to obey this commandment and resist those who break it.

Here belongs every kind of arrogance and disobedience.

Breaking the Fifth Commandment

Whoever is angry with his neighbor.

Whoever says to him, "Raca" [Matt. 5:22]—which represents any expression of anger and hatred.

Whoever says to him, you nitwit,[31] you fool [Matt. 5:22], that is, uses all sorts of insults, profanity, slander, backbiting, condemnation, scorn against his neighbor.

Whoever makes his neighbor's sin or shortcomings public and does not cover and excuse [these].

Whoever does not forgive his enemies, does not pray for them, is not friendly, and does them no kindness.

Breaking this commandment includes all sins of anger and hatred, such as murder, war, robbery, arson, quarreling and feuding, begrudging a neighbor's good fortune, and rejoicing over his misfortune [1 Cor. 13:6].

Whoever fails to practice merciful deeds even toward his enemies [Matt. 5:44; Rom. 12:20].

Whoever sets persons against one another and incites them to strife [Prov. 16:28].

Whoever causes disunity between persons.

Whoever does not reconcile those who are at odds with one another [Matt. 5:9].

Whoever does not prevent or forestall anger and discord wherever he can.

Breaking the Sixth Commandment

Whoever violates virgins, commits adultery, incest, and similar kinds of sexual sins.

Whoever commits sexual perversions (called the silent sins) [Rom. 1:26-27; Lev. 18:22-23; 20:10-16].

Whoever uses lewd words, ditties, stories, pictures to incite sexual lust or displays evil lust.

Whoever stirs up sexual desires in himself and contaminates himself by ogling, touching, and sexual fantasies.

Whoever does not avoid provocation to sexual sins—heavy drinking and eating, laziness and idleness, sleeping too much, and associating with persons of the opposite sex.

Whoever incites others to unchastity by excessive personal adornment, suggestive gestures, and other means.

Whoever allows his house, room, time, or assistance to be used for such sexual sins.

Whoever does not do and say what he can to help another person to be chaste.

31. Luther uses an old Latin term of scorn, *fatue*, from which the word *fatuous* is derived. Evidently the ancient epithet was still used in his time.

Breaking the Seventh Commandment

Whoever steals, robs, and practices usury.

Whoever uses short weights and measures [Deut. 25:15], or who passes off poor merchandise as good.

Whoever gets an inheritance or income by fraud.

Whoever withholds earned wages [Deut. 24:15] and whoever refuses to acknowledge his debts.

Whoever refuses to vouch for or lend money without interest to a needy neighbor.

All who are avaricious and want to get rich quickly.

Whoever in any way keeps what belongs to another or keeps for himself what is only entrusted to him for a time.

Whoever does not try to prevent loss to another person.

Whoever does not forewarn his neighbor against possible loss.

Whoever hinders what is advantageous to his neighbor.

Whoever is vexed by his neighbor's increase in wealth.

Breaking the Eighth Commandment

Whoever conceals and supresses the truth in court.

Whoever does harm by untruth and deceit.

Whoever uses flattery to do harm, or spreads gossip, or uses double-talk.

Whoever brings his neighbor's conduct, speech, life, or wealth into question or disrepute.

Whoever allows others to speak evil about his neighbor, helps them, and does nothing to oppose them.

Whoever does not speak up in defense of his neighbor's good repute.

Whoever does not take a backbiter to task.

Whoever does not speak well about all his neighbors and does not keep silent about what is bad about them.

Whoever conceals the truth or does not defend it.

Breaking the Last Two Commandments

The last two commandments set a goal or target which we should attain. Daily and penitently we must strive toward this goal with God's help and grace because our evil desires will not die completely until our flesh is reduced to dust and then created anew.

---

32. Luther in this paragraph refers to devices or lists that were commonly included in medieval prayer books and catechisms. He implicitly makes the point that these are unnecessary because everything important is included in the Ten Commandments. Luther rejects all these other lists and returns the Christian to the Ten Commandments.

33. Kolde (106) discusses seven works of physical mercy and seven works of spiritual mercy. The works of physical mercy are feeding the hungry, giving drink to the thirsty, freeing prisoners, visiting the sick, clothing the naked, sheltering pilgrims and other suffering people, and burying the dead.
The works of spiritual mercy are: "Counseling naïve and simple people. Teaching the ignorant. Punishing the sinful. Comforting the grieving. Forgiving those who have offended you. Enduring and tolerating for God's sake, those who are burdensome and annoying. Interceding for all faithful souls, hearing mass for them, giving alms, fasting, and praying for them."

The five senses are comprehended in the Fifth and Sixth Commandments;[32] the six works of mercy[33] in the Fifth and Seventh; the seven mortal sins[34]—pride in the First and Second, lust in the Sixth, wrath and hatred in the Fifth, gluttony in the Sixth, sloth in the Third, and, for that matter, in all of them. The alien sins[35] are covered by all the commandments, for it is possible to break all the commandments just by talking, advising, or helping someone. The crying and silent sins[36] are committed against the Fifth, Sixth, and Seventh Commandments. In all of these deeds we can see the same thing: love of self which seeks its own advantage, robs both God and one's neighbor of their due, and concedes neither to God nor man anything of what they have, or are, or could do or become. Augustine expressed this succinctly when he said, "Self-love is the beginning of every sin."

The conclusion of all this is that the commandments demand or forbid nothing other than love. Only love fulfills and only love breaks the commandments. Therefore St. Paul declares that "love is the fulfilling of the law" [Rom. 13:8-10], just as an evil love breaks all the commandments.

34. Arrogance (pride), greed, unchastity (lust), anger, gluttony, envy, idleness.

35. Kolde (68) discusses nine "alien" sins, that is, sins that involve the sin of others. These include such things as requiring others to sin, providing aid to the commission of sin, consenting to sin, praising sin, harboring and protecting thieves, murderers, etc., eating and drinking from ill-gotten wealth, and failing to prevent sin when one could do so.

36. Along with "openly discussed sins," Kolde includes a discussion (69–70) of "the mute sins against nature that are seldom or never discussed." Kolde comments that it "occurs in myriad ways, such as with thoughts, with touching, with women, with men, or in various self-indulgent and forsaken ways."

This seven-paneled painting (polyptych)
by Master of Alkmaar (1504)
depicts the seven works of charity.
Located in Museum Boijmans Van Beunigen,
on loan from the Rijksmuseum Amsterdam.

37. This presages how Luther explains the First Commandment in the *Small Catechism* (1529), namely, that we should "fear, love, and trust God above all things."

38. The German is *gottis diensten* (see p. 169, n. 26 above).

39. In other places, Luther's explanation of the Fourth Commandment also includes a discussion of the duties and obligations of those in authority. See, for example, the *Large Catechism*, in BC, 409–10 ; TAL 2:314–27..

Fulfilling the Commandments

The First

Fear and love God in true faith,[37] at all times, firmly trusting him in all that he does, accepting in simple, quiet confidence everything whether good or bad. What all of Scripture records about faith and hope and the love of God [1 Cor. 13:13] belongs here and is briefly comprehended in this commandment.

The Second

Praise, honor, glorify, and call upon God's name, and rather sink into utter nothingness so that God alone be exalted, who is in all things and works in everything [Rom. 8:28; 11:36; Eph. 4:6]. Here belongs all that Scripture teaches about giving praise, honor, and thanksgiving to God and rejoicing in God's name.

The Third

Yield to God so that all we do is done by him alone through us. This commandment requires us to be poor in spirit [Matt. 5:3], to sacrifice our nothingness to God so that God is our only God and that in us God's deeds may be glorified [2 Cor. 9:13] as the first two commandments require. Here belongs everything required of us: serving God,[38] listening to what is preached, doing good deeds, subjecting the body to the spirit [1 Cor. 9:27], so that all our works are God's and not our own.

The Fourth[39]

Show a willing obedience, humility, submissiveness to all authority as pleasing to God, as the Apostle St. Peter says [1 Pet. 2:13], without protesting, complaining, and murmuring. Here belongs all that is written regarding obedience, humility, submissiveness, and giving honor.

The Fifth

Patience, meekness, kindness, peacefulness, mercy, and in every circumstance a tender and friendly heart, devoid of all hatred, anger, and bitterness toward any person, even our enemies. Here belong all precepts concerning patience, meekness, peace, and harmonious relationships with others.

The Sixth

Chastity, decency, modesty in deeds, speech, attitude, and thought. Also moderation in eating, drinking, sleeping, and doing whatever encourages chastity. Here belong all precepts concerning chastity, fasting, sobriety, temperance, praying, being vigilant, working hard, and whatever else furthers chastity.

The Seventh

To be poor in spirit [Matt. 5:3], generous, willing to lend or give of our possessions, and to live free of avarice and covetousness. Here belongs all teaching about avarice, fraudulent gain, exploitative interest, deceit, craftiness, and allowing harm to happen to or hindering our neighbor's worldly goods.

The Eighth

A peaceful and beneficial manner of speech which harms no one and benefits everyone, reconciles the discordant, excuses and defends the maligned, that is, a manner of speech which is truthful and sincere. Here belong all precepts concerning when to keep silent and when to speak in matters affecting our neighbor's reputation, rights, concerns, and happiness.

The Last Two

They mean: perfect chastity and thorough disregard for all temporal pleasures and possessions—something not attainable until we reach the life beyond this one.

    In all such actions we see nothing but an alien, comprehensive love toward God and our neighbor that never seeks its own advantage but only what serves God and our neighbor [1 Cor. 13:5]. And devotes itself freely to belonging to one's neighbor and serving him and his concerns.

    Now you see that the Ten Commandments contain in a brief and orderly manner all precepts needful for a person's life.[40]

40. Luther emphasizes again that the Ten Commandments suffice—one does not need the various lists (of works of mercy, of various types of sin, etc.) common in medieval devotional works.

Anyone wishing to keep them all will find enough good deeds to do to fill every hour of the day; he need not hunt for other things to do, running here and there to do things which are not commanded.

We have clearly emphasized that these commandments prescribe nothing that a person is to do or leave undone for his own advantage, or expect of others for himself, but rather what a person is to do or leave undone toward others, toward God, and toward neighbor. Therefore we must comprehend the fulfillment of the commandments always as meaning love for others and not for ourselves. For a person is more than enough inclined to occupy himself with whatever benefits himself as things are. He needs no precepts for doing this, but needs rather to be restrained. The person who lives the best life does not live for himself; he who lives for himself lives the most dastardly kind of life. This is what the Ten Commandments teach, and they show us how few persons really live a good life, yes, that not one person is able to live this good life. Now that we recognize this, we must find out where to get the [medicinal] herbs to enable us to live a good life and fulfill the commandments.

Jesus

The Creed[41]

The Creed is divided into three main parts, each telling about one of the three persons of the holy divine Trinity.[42] The first—the Father; the second—the Son; and the third—the Holy Spirit. For this is the most important article in our faith, on which all the others are based.

Notice here that faith is exercised in two ways. First, a faith about God, meaning that I believe that what is said about God is true, just as I might say I believe that what people say about the Turks,[43] the devil, and hell is true. This kind of believing is more an item of knowledge or an observation than a creed. The second kind of faith means believing in God—not just that I believe that what is said about God is true, but that I put my trust in him, that I make the venture and take the risk to deal with him, believing beyond doubt that what God will be toward me or do with me will be just as they[q] say. I do not believe in this manner

41. The Apostles' Creed, the most common creed taught in western Europe in the medieval era.

42. Luther breaks with medieval tradition and discusses the Creed in terms of three parts, linking each to a member of the Trinity. Medieval works commonly discussed the Creed in twelve parts, linking each part to a particular apostle. By dropping from twelve to three, Luther not only simplifies the discussion but also puts the focus on the work of each member of the Trinity.

43. "Turks" may refer to people from the Ottoman Empire or to Muslims, the main religious group of the Ottoman Empire.

regarding any Turk or human being, no matter how highly he be praised. It is easy for me to believe that a certain man is outstandingly religious, but that is no reason for me to build [my life] upon him. Only a faith that ventures everything in life and in death on what is said of God makes a person a Christian and obtains all he desires from God.[44] No corrupt or hypocritical heart can have such a faith; this is a living faith as the First Commandment demands: I am your God; you shall have no other gods.

So that little word *in* is well chosen and should be noted carefully; we do not say, I believe God the Father, or I believe about the Father, but rather, I believe *in* God the Father, *in* Jesus Christ, in the Holy Spirit. And one should give this faith to no one except God alone and through it we confess the deity of Christ and of the Holy Spirit, thus believing in them just as we do in the Father. And just as there is one faith in all three Persons so the three Persons are one God.

The top portion of this 1511 painting by Albrecht Dürer (1471–1528) depicts God as Trinity. God the Father holds Christ the crucified Son, as the Holy Spirit as a dove flies above.

The First Part of the Creed

I believe in God, the Father almighty, maker of heaven and the earth. This means: I renounce the evil spirit, all idolatry, all sorcery, and all false belief.

I put my trust in no person on earth, not in myself, my power, my skill, my possessions, my piety, nor in anything else I may have.

I place my trust in no creature, whether in heaven or on earth.

I take the risk of placing my confidence only in the one, invisible, inscrutable, and only God, who created heaven and earth

44. Luther here discusses saving faith, contrasting it to mere intellectual knowledge.

q A reference to the Scriptures.

and who alone is superior to all creation. Again, I am not terrified by all the wickedness of the devil and his cohorts because God is superior to them all.

I would believe in God not a bit less if I were to be forsaken and persecuted by all people.

I would believe in God no less if I were poor, unintelligent, uneducated, despised, or lacking in everything.

I believe no less though I am a sinner. For this manner of faith will of necessity rise over all that does or does not exist, over sin and virtue and all else, thus depending purely and completely upon God as the First Commandment enjoins me to do.

I do not ask for any sign from God to put God to the test.

I trust in God steadfastly, no matter how long God may delay, and prescribe neither a goal, nor a time, nor a measure, nor a way [for God to respond to me], but leave all to God's divine will in a free, honest, and genuine faith.

If God is almighty, what could I lack that God could not give or do for me?

If God is the Creator of heaven and earth and Lord over every thing, who, then, could deprive me of anything, or do me harm [Rom. 8:31]? Yes, how can it be otherwise than that all things work for good for me [Rom. 8:28] if the God whom all creation obeys and serves is well intentioned toward me?

If God is God, God can and knows how to do what is best with me. Since God is Father, God will do all this and do it gladly.

And since I do not doubt this but place my trust in God, I am assuredly God's child, servant, and eternal heir, and it will be with me as I believe.

The Second Part

And in Jesus Christ, his only Son, our Lord: who was conceived by the Holy Spirit, born of the virgin Mary, suffered under Pontius Pilate, was crucified, dead, and buried: he descended into hell, the third day he rose from the dead, he ascended into heaven, and is seated at the right hand of God, the Father almighty, whence he shall come to judge the living and the dead.

I do not only believe that Jesus Christ is the one true Son of God, begotten of him in eternity with one eternal divine nature and essence—but I also believe that the Father has made all things subject to him, that according to his human nature he has been made one Lord over me and all things which he created together with the Father in his divinity.

I believe that no one can believe in the Father and that no one can come to him by any ability, deeds, understanding, or anything that may be named in heaven or on earth [Eph. 3:15] but only in and through Jesus Christ, his only Son, that is, through faith in his name and lordship.

I firmly believe that for my welfare Christ was conceived by the Holy Spirit, by no human or carnal act and without any physical father or seed of man, so that he gives me and all who believe in him a pure, spiritual being, cleansing me of my sinful, carnal, impure, damnable conception [Ps. 51:5]—all this through his and the Almighty Father's gracious will.

I believe that for my sake he was born of the immaculate Virgin Mary,[45] without changing her physical and spiritual virginity, so that according to his fatherly mercy he might render my sinful and damnable birth blessed, innocent, and pure, as he does for all his believers.

I believe that for my sin and the sin of all believers Christ bore his suffering and cross and thereby transformed all suffering and every cross into a blessing—doing [the believer] no harm and even being salutary and most beneficial.

I believe that Christ died and was buried to put my sin to death [2 Tim. 1:10] and bury it and do the same for all believers and, moreover, that he slew human death [1 Cor. 15:26], transforming it into something that does no harm and is beneficial [Phil. 1:10] and salutary.

I believe that for me and all his believers Christ descended into hell to subdue the devil [1 Pet. 3:18-20] and take him captive along with all his power, cunning, and malice so that the devil can no longer harm me, and that he redeemed me from the pains of hell, transforming them into something nondestructive and beneficial.

I believe that he was resurrected from the dead on the third day to give a new life to me and all believers, thus awakening us with him by his grace and spirit henceforth to sin no more [Rom. 6:4; Gal. 2:20] but to serve him only with every grace and virtue, thus fulfilling God's commandments.

I believe that he ascended into heaven and received power and honor over all angels and creatures [Phil. 2:9-10] and now sits at God's right hand [Eph. 1:20-22]. This means that he is King

45. Luther shared the medieval belief that Mary remained a virgin even after the birth of Jesus.

and Lord over all that is God's in heaven, earth, and hell. Hence he can help me and all believers against all troubles and against every adversary and foe [Rom. 8:38-39].

I believe that Christ will return from heaven on the Last Day to judge those who are alive at that time and those who have died before that day [1 Thess. 4:16-17], that all humankind, angels, and devils will have to appear before his judgment [Matt. 18:35; Rom. 14:10; 1 Pet. 1:17] throne to see him visually. Then he will redeem me and all who believe in him from bodily death and every infirmity and will eternally punish his enemies and adversaries and deliver us from their power forever [Rev. 20:11-14].

The Third Part

I believe in the Holy Spirit, one holy Christian church,[46] one communion of saints, one forgiveness of sins, resurrection of the body, and life everlasting. Amen.

I believe not only what this means—that the Holy Spirit is truly God together with the Father and the Son—but also that except through the Holy Spirit's work no one can come in and to the Father through Christ and his life, his suffering and death, and all that is said of him, nor can anyone appropriate any of this to himself. Working through the Spirit, Father and Son stir, awaken, call, and beget new life in me and in all who are his. Thus the Spirit in and through Christ quickens, sanctifies, and awakens the spirit in us and brings us to the Father, so that the Father through Christ and in Christ is active and life-giving everywhere.

I believe that throughout the whole wide world there is only one holy, universal, Christian church, which is nothing other than the gathering or congregation of saints—pious believers on earth. This church is gathered, preserved, and governed by the same Holy Spirit and is given daily increase by means of the sacraments and the word of God.

I believe that no one can be saved who is not in this gathering or community, harmoniously sharing with it in one faith, word, sacraments, hope, and love. And that no Jew, heretic, pagan, or sinner can be saved along with this community unless he becomes reconciled with it and unites with it in full agreement in all things.

I believe that in this community or Christendom all things

46. Luther continues the late medieval German tradition of translating the Latin *Catholicam* as "Christian" rather than "catholic" or "universal." See Albrecht Peters, *Commentary on Luther's Catechisms: Creed*, trans. Thomas H. Trapp (St. Louis: Concordia, 2011), 267–72.

This illustration depicts the church gathered around the word preached and the sacraments of Baptism and Eucharist.

are held in common; what each one possesses belongs also to others and no one has complete ownership of anything. Hence, all the prayers and good deeds of all the Christian community benefit, aid, and strengthen me and every other believer at all times, both in life and in death, and that each one bears the other's burden, as St. Paul teaches [Gal. 6:2].

I believe that there is forgiveness of sin nowhere else than in this community and that beyond it nothing can help to gain it—no good deeds, no matter how many or how great they might be; and that within this community nothing can invalidate this forgiveness of sin—no matter how gravely and often one may sin; and that such forgiveness continues as long as this one community exists. To this [community] Christ gave the power of the keys,[47] saying in Matthew 18[:18], "Whatever you bind on earth shall be bound in heaven." He said the same to Peter as an individual, representing and taking the place of the one and only one church, "Whatever you bind on earth," etc., Matthew 16[:18-19].

I believe that there will be a resurrection from the dead in the future in which all flesh will be raised from the dead through the Holy Spirit, that is, all humankind, good and evil, will be raised bodily to return alive in the same flesh in which they died, were buried, and decayed or perished in various ways.

I believe that after the resurrection the saints will have eternal life and the sinners eternal dying. And I do not doubt all this, that the Father through his Son Jesus Christ our Lord and with the Holy Spirit will let all this happen to me. Amen, that is, this is a sure and trustworthy truth.

The Lord's Prayer

*Preface and Preparation
for Praying the Seven Divine Petitions*

Our Father who art in heaven
What this means:
O Almighty God, in your unmerited[48] goodness to us and through the merit and mediation of your only beloved Son, our Lord Jesus Christ, you have not only permitted but also commanded and taught us to regard you and call upon you as one Father of

47. Luther's assertion that the keys are given to the community directly contradicts the Roman view that Christ gave the keys to the disciple Peter and through him to his successors, the popes.

48. The German *grundlossz* has the double meaning of "unmerited" and "bottomless" or "unfathomable."

Jesus teaches his disciples
about prayer (Luke 11:1–13).

49. Luther's description of the child calling on the father here contrasts sharply with other medieval descriptions of prayer. Kolde (87) tells his readers they should ask in three ways: "First, you should ask as a criminal who asks the judge not to sentence him to death. Second, you should ask as a poor man asking a rich lord for gifts and possessions. Third, you should ask as a dear child fondly asks his dear father."

us all. You have done so although instead you could rightly and properly be a severe judge over us sinners since we have acted so often and gravely against your divine and good will and have aroused your wrath. Now through this same mercy implant in our hearts a comforting trust in your fatherly love, and let us experience the most sweet and pleasant savor of a childlike certainty that we may joyfully call you Father, knowing and loving you and calling on you in every trouble.[49] Watch over us that we may remain your children and never become guilty of making you, dearest Father, our fearful judge, and making ourselves, your children, into your foes.

You do not wish us just to call you Father but that we all, together, should call on you, Our Father, and so harmoniously pray for all. Therefore grant us a harmonious love so that we may all regard and accept each other as true brothers and sisters and turn to you as the dear Father of us all, praying for all persons as one child might entreat his father for someone else. Let us not seek only our own advantage in prayer before you, forgetting the other person, but let us strip ourselves of all hatred, envy, and discord, and love each other as true pious children of God, and thus all repeat together not *my* Father, but *our* Father.

Moreover, since you are not a physical father here on earth but a spiritual Father in heaven, not like an earthly, mortal father who dies and is not always dependable and may not be able to help himself, show us what an immeasurably better Father you are and teach us to regard earthly fatherhood, fatherland, friends, possessions, body and blood as far less in value than you. Grant us, O Father, that we may be your heavenly children, and teach us to value only our spiritual and heavenly inheritance, lest an earthly father, fatherland, or earthly goods delude, catch, and hinder us and make us into merely children of this world. And grant that we might say with true conviction: O our heavenly Father, we are truly your heavenly children.

The First Petition

Hallowed be your name

What this means:

O Almighty God, dear heavenly Father, in this wretched vale of tears your holy name is sadly profaned, blasphemed, and reviled in so many ways. In so many instances it is regarded without honor to you and is often misused in many matters and in sinning, so that to live a disgraceful life might well be regarded as the same as disgracing and dishonoring your holy name.

Therefore grant us your divine grace that we might guard against all that does not serve to the honor and glory of your holy name. Help to do away with all sorcery and magic incantations. Help put an end to conjuring by the devil or other creatures by your name. Help root out all false belief and superstition. Help bring to naught all heresies and false doctrines that are spread under the guise of your name. Help that no one be deceived by the many kinds of falsehood that go under the pretense of truth, piety, and holiness. Help that no one may use your name to swear, lie, or deceive. Protect us from all false and imaginary consolation that might be given in your name. Protect us against all spiritual arrogance and false pride based on temporal fame or reputation. Help us to call upon your holy name in all our troubles and infirmities. Help us not to forget your name when we lie on our deathbed and our conscience is troubled. Help that we may use all our possessions, speech, and deeds to glorify and honor you alone and that we do not seek to claim or seek a reputation in doing this, but that all we do be done for you to whom alone everything belongs. Protect us from the shameful vice of ingratitude.

Help that our good deeds and conduct may incite others to praise not us, but you in us and to honor your name. Help so that our evil actions and shortcomings may not offend anyone, leading them to dishonor your name or to neglect your praise. Protect us from asking you for anything temporal or eternal which would not serve the glory and honor of your name. Should we petition you in such a way, do not listen to our folly. Help us conduct all our life in such a way that we may be found to be true children of God, so that your fatherly name is not named among us falsely or in vain. Amen.

And in this prayer belong all psalms and prayers in which one praises, honors, sings, and thanks God and every alleluia.

The Second Petition

May your kingdom come near[50]

What this means:

This wretched life is a realm[51] of every sin and malice, whose

50. Luther's German reads *zukomme dein Reich. Zukommen* means "to approach," "to come near," or "to send forward."

51. The German here is *Reich,* or "kingdom."

one lord is the evil spirit, the initiator and villainous instigator of all sin and wickedness. Yours is a realm, however, of every virtue and grace, whose one Lord is Jesus Christ, your dear Son, the Author and Beginner of every grace and truth. For this, dear Father, give us help and grace. Above all else grant us a true and constant faith in Christ, a fearless hope in your mercy overcoming all the stupidity of our sinful conscience, and a kindly love toward you and all people.

Protect us from unbelief, despair, and from boundless envy. Deliver us from the filthy lust of unchastity and grant us a love of every kind of virginity and chastity. Deliver us from discord, war, and dissension, and let the virtue, peace, harmony, and tranquility of your kingdom draw near. Help us that anger or other bitterness may not reign over us, but that by your grace, genuine kindness, loyalty, and every kind of friendliness, generosity, and gentleness may reign in us. Grant that inordinate sadness and depression may not prevail in us, but let joy and delight in your grace and mercy come over us. And finally may all sins be averted from us and, being filled with your grace and with all virtues and good deeds, may we become your kingdom so that in heart,[52] feeling, and thought we may serve you with all our strength inwardly and outwardly, obediently serving your commandments and will, being governed by you alone and not following self-love, the flesh, the world, or the devil.

Help that your kingdom, begun in us, may daily increase and improve, lest cunning malice and apathy for doing good overcome us so that we slip back. Rather grant us both an earnest resolve and an ability not only to begin to live a pious life but also to make vigorous progress in it and reach its goal. As the prophet says, "Lighten my eyes, lest I sleep the sleep of death or become slothful in the good life I have begun, and my enemy again have power over me."[r]

Help, that we may thus remain steadfast and that your future kingdom may be the end and consummation of the kingdom you have begun. Help us get free from this sinful and perilous life. Help us to yearn for that future life and be an enemy of this

52. "Heart" for Luther includes both reason and emotion, that is, he does not share the modern tendency to let "heart" refer merely to the emotions. "For Luther, thought is intimately connected to emotion. The mutual connection between thought and emotion is a major presupposition of Luther's anthropology. . . . This classic conception of the human heart has a very wide range of meaning from thinking to feeling. Today, the metaphorical sense of 'heart' is restricted to mere 'feeling.'" Birgit Stolt, "Luther's Faith of 'the Heart,'" in Christine Helmer, ed., *The Global Luther: A Theologian for Modern Times* (Minneapolis: Fortress Press, 2009), 135. See also Birgit Stolt, *"Lasst uns fröhlich springen!" Gefühlswelt und Gefühlsnavigierung in Luthers Reformationsarbeit* (Berlin: Weidler, 2012), esp. 252–54.

r   Psalm 13:3b-4. To this passage, Luther added "become slothful in the good life I have begun."

present life. Help us not to fear death but to desire it. Turn us from love and attachment to this life so that in everything your kingdom may be accomplished in us.

And in this petition belong all psalms, verses, and prayers that implore God for grace and virtue.

The Third Petition

Your will be done on earth as it is in heaven

What this means:

Compared with your will, our will is never good but always evil. Your will is at all times the best, to be cherished and desired above everything else. Therefore have mercy upon us, O dear Father, and let nothing happen just because it is our own will. Grant and teach us a deep patience in times when our will is prevented from happening or comes to nothing. Help when others contradict our will by what they say or do not say, do or leave undone, that we not become angry or vexed, not curse, complain, protest, condemn, disparage, or contradict. Help us to yield humbly to our adversaries and those who obstruct our will, surrendering our own will so that we praise, bless, and do good to these adversaries as persons who are carrying out your best and godly purposes in contradiction to our own.

Grant us grace to bear willingly all sorts of sickness, poverty, disgrace, suffering, and adversity and to recognize that in this your divine will is crucifying our will. Help us also to endure injustice gladly and preserve us from taking revenge. Let us not repay evil with evil [Matt. 5:39; Rom. 12:19, 21] nor meet violence with violence, but rather let us rejoice that these things happen to us according to your will and so let us praise and give thanks to you [Matt. 5:11]. Let us not ascribe to the devil or to evil persons anything that happens contrary to our will, but solely ascribe this to your divine will which orders everything that may hinder our will in order to increase the blessedness of your kingdom. Help us to die willingly and gladly and readily accept death as your will so that we do not become disobedient to you through impatience or discouragement.

Grant that we do not give our bodily members—eyes, tongue, heart, hands, and feet—free rein for what they desire or purpose, but make them captive to your will, bring them to a stop, and subdue them. Protect us from any kind of evil will—rebellious, stubborn, stiff-necked, obstinate, or capricious. Grant us true obedience, a perfect, calm, single-minded composure in all things—spiritual, earthly, temporal, and eternal. Protect us from the horrible vice of character assassination, from slander, backbiting, frivolously judging, condemning others, and misrepresenting what others have said. O hold far from us the plague and tragedy that such speech can cause; rather, whenever we see or hear anything in others that seems wrong or displeasing to us, teach us to keep quiet, not to publicize it, and to pour out our complaints to you alone and to commit all to your will. And so let us sincerely forgive all who wrong us and be sympathetic toward them.

Teach us to recognize that none can harm us without first harming themselves a thousand times more in your eyes, so that we might thus be moved more to pity rather than to anger toward such persons, to commiserate with them rather than to count up their wrongs. Help us to refrain from rejoicing whenever those who did not do our will or did us harm in their conduct are struck with adversity or other misfortune in their lives. Also help us not to be saddened by their good fortune.

To this petition belongs every psalm, verse, or prayer which petitions for help against sin and our foes.

The Fourth Petition

Give us this day our daily bread

What this means:

This bread is our Lord Jesus Christ who feeds and comforts the soul [John 6:51].[53] Therefore, O heavenly Father, grant grace that the life, words, deeds, and suffering of Christ be preached, made known, and preserved for us and all the world. Help that we may find in his words and deeds a powerful example and mirror of all virtues for all of life. Help that we may be strengthened and comforted in suffering and adversity in and through his suffering and cross. Help that we through his death overcome our own death with a firm faith and thus boldly follow our beloved Guide into the life beyond this one.

Graciously grant that all pastors preach your word and Christ throughout the world in a way effective for salvation. Help that all who hear the preaching of your word may learn to know Christ and thus sincerely lead better lives. May you also

53. This explanation of the fourth petition does not relate "daily bread" to bodily needs as does the explanation in the *Small Catechism*. Medieval interpretations often gave "bread" a spiritual meaning, including an understanding of "bread" as the bread of the Lord's Supper. Luther appropriated and changed this tradition. In his early works he understood "bread" as the Word of God, or Christ. See Paul W. Robinson, "Luther's Explanation of Daily Bread in Light of Medieval Preaching," *Lutheran Quarterly* (NS) 13 no. 4 (Winter 1999), 435–47.

graciously drive out of the holy church all foreign doctrine and preaching that do not teach Christ.

Be merciful to all bishops, priests, other clergy, and to all in authority that illumined by your grace they may teach and lead us correctly through speech and good example.

Protect all who are weak in faith that they may not be offended by the bad example set by those in authority.

Protect us against heretical and apostate teachers[54] so that we may remain united in one daily bread—the daily teaching and word of Christ. Teach us by your grace to contemplate Christ's suffering in a proper manner, to take it to heart and rejoice to copy it in our lives. Let us not be deprived of the holy and true body of Christ at our final end. Help all priests to administer and use the sacred sacrament worthily and blessedly for the betterment of all Christendom. Help that we and all Christians blessedly receive the holy sacrament with grace at the proper time.

And in summary, give us our daily bread so that Christ may remain in us eternally and we in him [John 15:5], and that we may worthily bear the name of Christian as derived from Christ.[55]

In this petition belong all prayers or psalms offered for those in authority and especially those directed against false teachers, those for the Jews, heretics, and all persons who err, those also for the grief-stricken and those who suffer without hope.

The Fifth Petition

And do not hold us accountable for our sins, as we do not hold accountable those who sin against us

What this means:

This petition has one supplement and condition: we must first forgive those who sin against us. When we have done that, then we may say, "Forgive us our sins." That is what we prayed for earlier in the Third Petition—that God's will be done, the will that one should endure everything with patience and not repay evil with evil, not seek revenge, but give good for evil as our Father in heaven does, who lets his sun rise on the pious and the evil and sends rain to those who thank him and to those who do not [Matt. 5:45]. Therefore we implore you, O Father, comfort us in the present and in the hour of our death[56] when

54. Luther probably had in mind here not only his Roman Catholic opponents but also those who claimed to follow him but, to his way of thinking, had taken his thinking in directions he did not intend.

55. Albrecht Peters traces the change in Luther's understanding of "bread" in the fourth petition. Prior to 1523, Luther understood "bread" as Christ, the bread of life, the food for the soul; beginning in 1523 he gives physical bread a broader place and by 1528 actual bread, the meeting of physical needs, is paramount. See Albrecht Peters, *Commentary on Luther's Catechisms: Lord's Prayer*, trans. Daniel Thies (St. Louis: Concordia, 2011), 124–30. See also Rudolf Dellsperger, "Unser tägliches Brot . . . Die Brotbitte bei Erasmus von Rotterdam, Martin Luther, Wolfgang Musculus und Petrus Canisius SJ," in Emidio Campi, Leif Grane, and Adolf Martin Ritter, eds., *Oratio: Das Gebet in patristischer und reformatorischer Sicht* (Göttingen: Vandenhoeck & Ruprecht, 1999), 211–26.

56. Here Luther understands the petition to be asking God to console us when we die. Much medieval devotional literature was intended to console the dying and help them take proper actions to prepare for death.

our conscience is and will be frightened terribly by our sins and by your judgment.

Grant your peace in our hearts that we may anticipate your judgment with joy. Let us not feel the harshness of your judgment, for no one could then be found righteous before you [Ps. 143:2]. Teach us, dear Father, not to rely on or find consolation in our good deeds or in merit, but simply to venture all upon your boundless mercy, committing ourselves with utter firmness to it alone. Likewise, let not our guilty and sinful life bring us into despair, but rather let us regard your mercy as higher, broader, and stronger than anything in our lives.

Help all who in peril of death and times of temptation are frightened by despair, particularly those whom we name. Have mercy upon all poor souls in purgatory, especially those we name [in our prayer]. Forgive them and all of us our sins, comfort them, and take them under your mercy.

Repay our wickedness with your goodness, as you have commanded us to do [to others]. Silence that evil spirit—the cruel backbiter, accuser, and magnifier of our sin—now and in our last hour, and in every torment of conscience, just as we, on our part, hold back from backbiting and magnifying the sins of others. Do not judge us according to the accusations of the devil or our wretched conscience, and pay no heed to the voice of our enemies who accuse us day and night before you, just as in turn we will pay no heed to the backbiters and accusers of others.

Relieve us of every heavy burden of sin and conscience so that we may live and die, suffer and conduct ourselves with a light and happy heart in complete confidence of your mercy.

In this petition belong all psalms and prayers which invoke God's mercy for our sin.

The Sixth Petition

And lead us not into temptation

What this means:

Three temptations or trials confront us: the flesh, the world, and the devil. Hence we pray: Dear Father, grant us grace that we may overcome fleshly lusts. Help that we may withstand excesses in eating and drinking, sleeping too much, idleness, and laziness. Help us through fasting, moderation in food, dress, and sleep, waking and working, to become serviceable and skilled in good works. Help us, with Christ, to crucify and put to death the evil inclination to unchastity and all of its desires and entice-ments [Rom. 6:6] that we may not yield to any temptations of the flesh or follow them. Help that when we look at a beautiful person or picture or any other creature, that this may not bring us into temptation but rather be an occasion for cherishing chas-tity and praising you in your creatures. Help that when we hear something pleasant or feel something pleasurable that we do not seek to indulge our lust in this but rather seek to praise and glo-rify you for it.

Protect us from the great vice of avarice and covetousness with regard to the riches of this world. Protect us from seeking honor and power in this world, or from even being inclined in this direction. Protect us that the deceit, delusion, and entice-ment of this world may not stir us to follow them. Keep us that we be not drawn into impatience, vindictiveness, anger, or other vices by the world's evil and unpleasantness.

Help us to renounce and forsake the world's deceit and delu-sion, promises and fickleness—all its good or evil—as we vowed to do in baptism. Help that we may remain steadfast and grow daily in [the promise of our baptism].

Protect us from the devil's whisperings so that we do not give in to pride, our own pleasure, and a contempt for others in order to gain wealth, high rank, power, skill, beauty, or any other good gift of yours. Protect us that we may not fall into hatred or envy for any reason whatsoever. Protect us that we may not fall victim to temptation of faith and despair, now and at our last hour.

Heavenly Father, may all who work and struggle against these great and manifold temptations be committed to your care. Strengthen those who are unbowed, raise up those who have fallen and are defeated. And give us all your grace, that we in the wretched insecurities of this life, being surrounded con-stantly by so many foes, may do battle with a firm and valiant faith, and may obtain an eternal crown.

The Seventh Petition

But deliver us from evil
What this means:
This petition bids for deliverance from every evil of pain and punishment, as the holy church does in the litanies. Deliver us,

O Father, from your eternal wrath and from the pangs of hell. Deliver us, O Father, in death and on Judgment Day, from your severe condemnation. Deliver us from sudden death. Protect us from fire and flood, from lightning and hail. Protect us from hunger and inflation. Protect us from war and bloodshed. Protect us from your plagues, pestilence, venereal disease, and other grave sickness. Protect us from every bodily evil and woe, to the end, that your name may be honored, your kingdom increased, and your divine will accomplished. Amen.

Amen

God grant that we may obtain all these petitions with certainty. Let us not doubt that you have heard us in the past and will do so in the future, answering us with a Yes and not a No or a Maybe. So we cheerfully say Amen—this is true and certain. Amen.

The Hail Mary[57]

Take note of this: no one should put his trust or confidence in the Mother of God or in her merits, for such confidence is worthy of God alone and is the lofty service due only to him.[58] Rather praise and thank God through Mary and the grace given her. Laud and love her simply as the one who, without merit, obtained such blessings from God, sheerly out of his mercy, as she herself testifies in the Magnificat [Luke 1:46-55].

It is very much the same when I, viewing the heavens, the sun, and all creation, am moved to praise the creator of all these and say: O God, Author of such a beautiful and perfect creation, grant to me. . . . Similarly, our prayer should include the Mother of God and say: O God, what a noble person you have created in her! May she be blessed! And so on. And you who honored her so highly, grant also to me . . . etc.

Let not our hearts cling to her in faith, but through her penetrate to Christ and to God himself. Thus what the Hail Mary says is that all glory should be given to God, using these words: "Hail, Mary, full of grace. The Lord is with you [Luke 1:28]; blessed are you among women and blessed is the fruit of thy body, Jesus Christ. Amen."

You see that these words are not concerned with prayer but purely with giving praise and honor, just as in the first words of

57. Luther includes one of the most common elements of medieval piety, the Hail Mary. Mary was seen as a patron of childbirth. But her appeal was broader. By the late Middle Ages, regional church synods were mandating that the Hail Mary be taught and recited, along with the Lord's Prayer and the Creed. It was considered one of the basic prayers of the church for both clergy and lay. See, for example, Anne L. Clark, "The Cult of the Virgin Mary and Technologies of Christian Formation," in John Van Engen, ed., *Educating People of Faith* (Grand Rapids: Eerdmans, 2004), 227–39.

58. Luther immediately makes a statement about how Mary is to be regarded. Rejecting medieval views that encourage prayer to Mary and even see her as a mediator between God and humans, he encourages an evangelical view of Mary. Luther's inclusion of the Hail Mary in his prayer book is another example of Luther taking a common element of medieval piety and, rather than rejecting it outright, giving it an evangelical interpretation.

the Lord's Prayer there is also no prayer but rather praise and glory to God, that he is our Father and is in heaven. Therefore we should make the Hail Mary neither a prayer nor an invocation because it is improper for us to interpret the words beyond what they mean in themselves and beyond the meaning given them by the Holy Spirit.

But there are two things we can do. First, we can use the Hail Mary as a meditation in which we recite what grace God has given her. Second, we can add a wish that everyone may know and respect her [as one blessed by God].

In the first place, she is full of grace, so that she is known as entirely without sin—something exceedingly great. For God's grace fills her with everything good and makes her devoid of all evil.

In the second place, God is with her, meaning that all she does or leaves undone is divine and the action of God in her. Moreover, God guards and protects her from all that might be hurtful to her.

In the third place, she is blessed above all other women, not only because she gave birth without labor, pain, and injury to herself, not as Eve and all other women, but because by the Holy Spirit and without sin, she became fertile, conceived, and gave birth in a way granted to no other woman.

In the fourth place, her [bodily] fruit is blessed in that it is spared the curse upon all children of Eve who are conceived in sin [Ps. 51:5] and born to deserve death and damnation. But only the fruit of her body is blessed, and through the same we are all blessed.

Furthermore, a prayer or wish is to be added, so that one prays for all who speak evil against this Fruit and the Mother. But who is it that speaks evil of this Fruit and the Mother? All who persecute and speak evil against his word, the gospel, and the faith, as Jews and papists are now doing.

From the above it follows that in the present no one speaks evil of this Mother and her Fruit as much as those who bless her

Madonna under the Fir Tree by
Lucas Cranach the Elder (1510)

59. Luther was very familiar with medieval Marian piety. We know that he read a devotional work (*Marienpsalter*) containing the rosary. His marginal notes indicate his doubts about claims made about the rosary's antiquity as well as his complaint that, instead of being pointed to Christ, humans are left to rely on their own works. See D. G. Kawerau, "Luthers Randglossen zum Marienpsalter 1515," *Theologische Studien und Kritiken* 80 (1917): 81–87.

60. Luther appended the German texts of eight psalms at this point in his prayer book. Only the psalm numbers and Luther's captions are given in our translation. There seems to be no readily apparent reason for choosing these eight psalms. It may be that Luther chose these in place of the penitential psalms in some prayer books and as psalms which stated the most needed emphases of Christian prayer, as the captions Luther wrote seem to indicate.

61. Just a few years later, Luther used Psalms 12 and 67 as the bases for two of his early hymns: "Ach Gott vom Himmel sieh darein . . ." (Psalm 12; LW 53:225–28) and "Es wollt uns Gott gnädig sein . . ." (Psalm 67; LW 53:232–34; WA 10/2:339).

with many rosaries and constantly mouth the Hail Mary. These, more than any others, speak evil against Christ's word and faith in the worst way.[59]

Therefore, notice that this Mother and her Fruit are blessed in a twofold way—bodily and spiritually. [Those who bless her] bodily with lips and the words of the Hail Mary blaspheme and speak evil of her most dangerously. And [those who bless her] spiritually in their hearts praise and bless her child, Christ in all his words, deeds, and sufferings. No one does this except the one who has the true Christian faith because without such faith no heart is good but is naturally stuffed full of evil speech and blasphemy against God and all the saints. For that reason the one who has no faith is advised to refrain from saying the Hail Mary and all other prayers. For it is written of such people: *Oratio eius fiat ynn peccatum*: Let his prayer be sin [Ps. 109:7].

Psalm 12[60]
To be prayed for the exaltation of the holy gospel

Psalm 67[61]
To be prayed for the increase of faith

Psalm 51
Concerning the whole matter, that is, the essential [matter] and original sin together with its fruits

Psalm 103
For thanking God for all his goodness

Psalm 20
For good government and for earthly authorities

Psalm 79
Against the enemies of the Christian church and the gospel

Psalm 25
A general prayer to submit to God in all things

Psalm 10
To be prayed against the Antichrist and his kingdom

The Epistle of St. Paul to Titus [62]

To give instruction for living a Christian life

Preface to St. Paul's Epistle to Titus [5]

This letter is a brief but finely formed model for Christian instruction, in which a number of things are masterfully discussed, that a Christian needs to know and to live. In the first chapter he [St. Paul] teaches what kind of person a bishop or pastor should be—namely, pious and educated for preaching the gospel and for refuting the false teaching of [salvation by] works and human precepts which continually do battle against faith and lead a person's conscience away from Christian liberty into the prison of their human works, which, after all, are vain.

In the second chapter he [St. Paul] instructs persons in all situations of life—the old and the young, women and men, masters and servants—how to conduct themselves as those whom Christ has won through his death to be his own.

In the third chapter he [St. Paul] teaches [us] to honor and obey governmental authorities in this world and calls attention again to the grace which Christ has gained for us, lest anyone think that obedience to the government suffices because before God all our righteousness amounts to nothing. And he commands us to shun those who are stubborn and heretics.

[Here Luther appended his German text of the Epistle to Titus.]

62. Luther included a translation of Titus in the earliest editions. The text (not translated here) shows some variations from the version that appeared later that year in his translation of the New Testament (the *September Testament*), indicating that he polished the text after he translated it for his prayer book. Later editions of the prayer book included that revised text.

5   The preface for Titus was added in the fifth printing of 1522. It was the same preface Luther wrote for use in his *September Testament* (1522).

63. Luther's *Passional* did not appear in the 1522 edition on which our prayer book translation is based. It was first printed in the Wittenberg edition of 1529. His substitute for the traditional passion history of the old prayer books with their legends about the Virgin Mary and the saints was a collection of fifty full-page woodcuts to illustrate stories from the Bible ranging from the creation to the last judgment. Under each woodcut Luther placed a title and a brief biblical text (indicated by the Bible references given). The selection of subject matter is significant because it indicates what Luther thought was important for a layperson to know about the Bible and to use for personal edification. In editions after 1529 woodcuts from Dürer's *Short Passion History* were substituted.

64. Luther's focus on teaching the biblical story here stands in contrast to medieval uses of the passion story. The popular late medieval prayer book *Hortulus animae* ("Garden of the Soul") contained many prayers focusing on the passion of Christ: "A description of the contents of the 1530 edition . . . [includes] the hours of the passion of Christ attributed to Bonaventure, a prayer entitled the 'golden passional,' a prayer attributed to Ambrose about each of the 'articles' of the passion of Christ, an abbreviated version of the said prayer, a prayer attributed to the Venerable Bede based on the seven last words of Christ and a prayer hailing the five wounds of Christ. This section of prayers concludes with the text of the passion according to John, which in turn is followed by the seven penitential psalms and the litany to the saints." See Reinis, *Reforming the Art of Dying*, 40.

65. Christ's passion was one of the key devotional themes of the late Middle

Passional[63]

Martin Luther[64]

I thought it expedient to add to the *Little Prayer Book* the old "Passional"[65] especially for the sake of children and simple people who are more apt to retain the divine stories when taught by picture and parable than merely by words or instruction. As St. Mark testifies,[t] Christ also preached in ordinary parables for the sake of simple folk.[u]

I have added some more stories from the Bible along with sayings from the text so that both may be retained more firmly. I hope that this may mark a beginning and set an example for others to follow and to improve upon as their talents allow.[66]

I do not think it wrong to paint such stories along with the verses on the walls of rooms and chambers so that one might have God's words and deeds constantly in view and thus encourage fear and faith toward God.[67] And what harm would there be if someone were to illustrate the important stories of the entire Bible in their proper order for a small book which might become known as a layman's Bible? Indeed, one cannot bring God's words and deeds too often to the attention of the common people. Even if concerning God's word, one sings and speaks, lets resound and preaches, writes and reads, and paints and draws it, Satan with his angels and cohorts is always strong and alert to hinder and suppress God's word. Hence our project and concern are not only useful, but necessary—in fact, very badly needed.

I don't care if the iconoclasts condemn and reject this.[68] They do not need our teaching and we don't want theirs, so it is easy for us to part company. I have always condemned and criticized the misuse of [religious] pictures and the false confidence placed in them and all the rest. But whatever is no misuse of pictures I

---

t   Mark 4:11.

u   For a study of attempts to convey Reformation theology on a popular level, see Robert Scribner, *For the Sake of Simple Folk: Popular Propaganda for the German Reformation* (Cambridge: Cambridge University Press, 1981).

The crucifixion of Jesus for 1550 printing
of *Hortulus animae*. In the background,
two scenes are depicted as foreshadowing
this event. On the right, Israelites in the wilderness
gaze upon the bronze serpent lifted on a cross.
On the left, an angel prevents Abraham
from sacrificing his son Isaac.
The monogrammist A.W. has left his mark
at the lower left corner.

———————————

Ages. Much art and various forms of literature were devoted to it. See, for example, Richard Kieckhefer, "Major Currents in Late Medieval Devotion," in Jill Raitt, ed., in collaboration with Bernard McGinn and John Meyendorff, *Christian Spirituality: High Middle Ages and Reformation* (New York: Crossroad, 1987), 83–89.

66. Luther encourages here solely the use of Bible stories—not the legends of the saints or the Virgin Mary, which were popular motifs of various forms of medieval art. More generally on Luther, art, and the Reformation, see Carl C. Christensen, *Art and the Reformation in Germany* (Athens: Ohio University Press, 1979).

67. Robert Scribner notes, "Protestant supporters of images, such as Luther, recognized the cognitive value of pictures for the education of pious Christians and strove to create a link between images and word. Iconophobes such as Zwingli denied this possibility: the pious Christian should know God with his or her heart only." Robert Scribner, "Perceptions of the Sacred in Germany," in Roper, ed., *Religion and Culture*, 97.

68. In this paragraph, Luther rejects iconoclastic views. Iconoclasts (destroyers of images) had claimed that images should not be used by Christians because they led to idolatry. Luther had returned from the Wartburg in early 1522 to stop reform moves that included the destruction of images. Luther saw clearly that, though images could be misused, they could also be used for the building up of faith. See also pp. 10–11 in this volume.

69. Just four examples of the forty-nine woodcuts in the 1529 Wittenberg printing of *Little Prayer Book* are included below.

have always permitted and encouraged their retention for beneficial and edifying results. This is the way we teach our common people; those clever fellows shall be neither our pupils nor our masters. May Christ be with all who believe in him and love him. Amen.

[Here followed the woodcuts with Luther's captions].⁶⁹

God creates the world (Gen. 1:1, 31; 2:2)

God created the world. Gen. 1:1, 31; 2:2.

God blows breath into Adam and creates Eve. Gen. 1:27; 2:22-23.

Eve offers an apple to Adam. Gen. 2:10-17; 3:4-5.

Expulsion from the Garden of Eden. Gen. 3:15.

Noah's ark. Gen. 6:5-6; 7:17, 23.

Destruction of Sodom. Gen. 18:20; 19:24-25.

Eating the first Passover meal. Exod. 12:3, 5-6.

Pharaoh drowns in the Red Sea. Exod. 14:27-29.

Moses receives the tables of the law. Exod. 20:1-2; Deut. 4:13.

Rain of manna. Exod. 16:14-15; Deut. 8:3.

The bronze serpent. Num. 21:8; John 3:14-15.

The annunciation of Mary. Isa. 7:14; Luke 1:30-31.

Mary and Elizabeth. Luke 1:39-56.

The birth of Christ. Luke 2:6-7.

Circumcision [of the Infant Jesus]. Luke 2:21.

Adoration of the Magi. Matt. 2:1-3, 11.

Slaughter of the infants [in Bethlehem]. Matt. 2:10-18.

Twelve-year-old Jesus in the Temple. Luke 2:43, 46, 49.

John [the Baptist] preaching. John 1:6-7; Luke 3:3.

Baptism of Christ. Matt. 3:13, 16-17.

Temptation [of Jesus]. Matt. 4:1, 4, 7, 10.

Marriage feast at Cana. John 2:2-3, 10.

Death of John [the Baptist]. Matt. 14:6-11.

Healing of the blind man and raising of Lazarus.
   Luke 18:35, 38; John 11:25-26, 43-44.

Entry on Palm Sunday. Matt. 21:5, 8-9.

Jesus washes the disciples' feet. John 13:4-5.

Lord's Supper. Luke 22:15, 19-20.

Gethsemane. Matt. 26:36ff.; Luke 22:43-44.

Arrest of Jesus. Matt. 26:47-56.

Jesus before Caiaphas. Mark 14:46, 53, 55.

Jesus before Pontius Pilate. Luke 22:66; 23:1, 3.

Scourging [of Jesus]. Luke 23:13, 16; John 19:1.

Soldiers crown Jesus. Matt. 27:27-31.

Pilate shows Jesus to the crowd. John 19:4-5.

Pilate washes his hands. Matt. 27:34-35.

Jesus carries his cross. Matt. 27:31; John 19:17.

Jesus is nailed to the cross. John 19:18-19.

Crucifixion. Luke 23:34, 46.

Jesus taken from the cross. Luke 23:50-53.

Jesus laid in the tomb. John 19:40-42.

Resurrection. Matt. 28:1-4.

The women at the grave. Matt. 28:5-7.

Jesus appears to Mary Magdalene. John 20:11-17.

Rain of manna
(Exod. 16:14 15; Deut. 8:3)

Gethsemane
(Matt. 26:36ff.; Luke 22:43-44)

Jesus shows himself to Thomas. John 20:26-27.

Ascension. Mark 16:14-19.

Outpouring of the Holy Spirit. Acts 2:1-4.

Baptism, preaching, and Lord's Supper in a church.
Mark 16:20; Acts 2:38, 41.

Christ as judge of the world. Matt. 26:64; 16:27.

Jesus commissions the disciples. Mark 16:15-16; Ps. 19:5.[70]

70. Rather than ending with the last judgment, Luther ends with a picture of messengers, sent two by two, armed with the story portrayed in the preceding forty-nine woodcuts. That story is not just for information; rather, it is "for you." Timothy J. Wengert, "Lutheran Missions," *Lutheran Quarterly* 29 (2015): 77–78. See the accompanying image.

Jesus commissions the disciples
(Mark 16:15–16; Ps. 19:5)

A Simple Way to Pray

How One Should Pray, For Peter, the Master Barber

1535

ERIC LUND

INTRODUCTION

During the Lenten season of 1517, only a few months before the posting of the *95 Theses*, Martin Luther preached a series of sermons in Wittenberg on the Lord's Prayer. These were published in April 1519 as *An Exposition of the Lord's Prayer for Simple Laymen.*[a] Sixteen years later, Luther returned to the same topic after being asked by his barber for advice about how to pray. Peter Beskendorf, also known as Peter Balbierer (the Barber), was a close friend of Luther. Luther already knew him in 1517, the year of the Lord's Prayer sermons, because he is mentioned then in a letter written to Christoph Scheurl, a jurist in Nuremberg.[1] Luther greeted him in several other letters and also made a reference to him in a sermon for the eighth Sunday after Trinity, which was published in the House Postil.[b] Peter had a reputation for being "a pious, God-fearing man who gladly listened to and discussed the word

1. Christoph Scheurl (1481–1542) taught canon law and human letters at the University of Wittenberg from 1507 to 1512. He then moved to Nuremberg where he served as legal advisor for the city until his death. He facilitated the publication of Luther's *95 Theses* in Nuremberg. A friend of both Luther and Luther's opponent Johann Eck (1486–1543) of Ingolstadt, he forwarded Luther's writings to the Catholic theologian, which stimulated their later debates.

---

a   *Auflegung deutsch des Vater unnser fuer dye einfeltigen leyen*; WA 2:74–130.
b   Eugene F. A. Klug, ed., *Sermons of Martin Luther: The House Postils*, trans. Erwin W. Koehlinger, James Lanning, and Everette W. Meier (Grand Rapids: Baker, 1996), 2:345; J. G. Walch, *Dr. Martin Luthers sämmtliche Schriften* (Jena, 1740–1753; reprint: St. Louis: Concordia, 1893), 21a:74; WA Br 1:108; WA Br 7:347; WA Br 8:200; WA 37:125.

253

of God.".[c] In response to his barber's request, Luther described how he himself prayed in *A Simple Way to Pray*.[d] As he had done in his sermons of 1517, Luther organized his comments around the seven petitions of the prayer Jesus taught to his disciples (Matt. 6:5-14; Luke 11:1-4).

Luther acknowledges at the start that it is not easy to sustain prayer meaningfully as a daily practice. People become lazy or listless and often get distracted by other mundane tasks that seem more urgent than prayer. Luther notes how Christ commanded prayer and taught both how and what to pray. In *A Simple Way to Pray*, Luther recommends his personal practice of beginning and ending the day with prayer and explicates a method of prayer based on the Lord's Prayer that is both elaborate and flexible. He humbly invites Peter and the readers of the pamphlet to adapt his approach to their own needs or even to improve on it if they can.

Jesus teaches his disciples about prayer (Matthew 6).

Several times in the years between 1517 and 1535, Luther also offered a commentary on the Lord's Prayer in conjunction with an analysis of the Ten Commandments and the Apostles' Creed. All three are treated as devotional texts in his *Little Prayer Book* published in 1522.[e] In that work and in the *Small Catechism* and *Large Catechism*[f] of 1529, Luther focuses first on the law (as summarized in the Ten Commandments), then on the gospel (as revealed in the Creed), and speaks of the Lord's Prayer as medi-

---

c   Walch, *Dr. Martin Luthers sämmtliche Schriften*, 9:1822.

d   LW 43:193–211; WA 38:358–75.

e   See pages 159–99 in this volume.

f   *Small Catechism*, see pp. 201–51 in this volume; *Large Catechism*, see TAL 2:279–416.

cine one might turn to after learning of the human predicament and the way to salvation. In *A Simple Way to Pray*, Luther also uses the Ten Commandments and the Creed as resources for prayer, but this time adds them as supplements to his initial focus on the Lord's Prayer. Luther's own practice is to combine prayer and meditation.[2] By focusing his mind, in succession, on each of the commandments and the three sections of the Creed, he sets out to "kindle a fire in the heart" and increase his eagerness for prayer. Considering what the Ten Commandments and the Creed reveal about God's will prompts him to offer thanks to God, confess his shortcomings, and finally ask for strength to incorporate what they teach into his life.

Within months of the writing of this piece, the life of Peter Beskendorf took a tragic turn. On the day before Easter, the barber was eating at the home of his daughter, Anna. His son-in-law, Dietrich, who had been a soldier, was apparently reporting on battles he had survived and boasting of his invulnerability to death. Peter, perhaps inebriated, put this to the test and stabbed Dietrich with his own sword at the dinner table. In the *Table Talk*, Luther once mentioned this shocking death and commented that the work of the devil must be behind it.[g] Luther intervened on behalf of his friend and managed to persuade the elector to banish him from Wittenberg instead of executing him. Peter relocated to Dessau, twenty-one miles away, where he had served earlier as barber/surgeon for Prince Joachim I of Anhalt-Dessau (1509–1561). He died in 1538.

A Simple Way to Pray was immediately popular and was printed four times during 1535, in Wittenberg, Nuremberg, and Augsburg. Altogether there were thirteen editions published during Luther's lifetime, including one in Low German and one in Latin.[h]

2. Luther's method bears traces of the *lectio divina* method that was used for the study of Scripture in a monastic setting. In the twelfth century a four-part practice became standardized as: reading, meditation, prayer, and contemplation. Luther later modified this practice and described the proper sequence for the study of theology, in the *Preface to the Wittenberg Edition of Luther's German Writings*, as: prayer, meditation, and testing (*oratio, meditatio, tentatio*); see pp. 477–78 and 482–88 in this volume; WA 50:657–61; LW 34:283–88. See John Kleinig, "The Kindled Heart: Luther on Meditation," *Lutheran Theological Journal* 20, nos. 2–3 (1986): 142–54; Martin Nicol, *Meditation bei Luther*, Forschungen zur Kirchen und Dogmengeschichte (Göttingen: Vandenhoeck & Ruprecht, 1984).

g   WA TR 3:70 (#4004)

h   See *Verzeichnis der im deutschen Sprachbereich erschienenen Drucke des 16. Jahrhunderts* (VD 16), at www.gateway-bayern.de/index_vd16.html.

3. The translation offered here is based on the German text in WA 38:358–75 (*Eine einfältige Weise zu beten für einen guten Freund*) and the English translation by Carl J. Schindler found in LW 43:193–211.

4. Peter the Barber is addressed as "Master" because of his senior guild status. A guild member started as an apprentice, became a journeyman, and then a "master."

5. Luther also refers to this state of mind in his *Large Catechism* (1529) when commenting on the Third Commandment. There he associates laziness or weariness with one of the traditional seven deadly sins, namely *acidia* (or *acedia*). He calls this "a malignant plague with which the devil bewitches and deceives many hearts so that he may take us by surprise and stealthily take the Word of God away again" (BC, 400; TAL 2:314). A long tradition of monastic reflection on the danger of this condition goes back to Evagrius Ponticus in the late fourth century.

6. A psalter is a book containing the Psalms and sometimes additional devotional material. Psalters were used in the Latin West from the early eighth century onward, especially by monastic communities, who chanted the Psalms daily. Luther first published a German edition of the book of Psalms in 1524. Over a hundred separate German psalter editions were printed in the sixteenth century. In his 1534 preface to the psalter Luther said the book "might well be called a Little Bible in which the whole Bible is beautifully and briefly collected, and compacted into an enchiridion or Manual" (LW 35:254, WA DB 10/1:100).

The Barber
by Lucas
van Leyden
(1494–1533)

A SIMPLE WAY TO PRAY [3]

HOW ONE SHOULD PRAY,
FOR PETER, THE MASTER BARBER [4]

DEAR MASTER PETER: I will tell you as best I can what I do personally when I pray. May our dear Lord grant to you and to everybody to do it better than I! Amen.

First, when I feel that I have become cold and listless[5] in prayer because of other tasks or thoughts (for the flesh and the devil always impede and obstruct prayer), I take my little psalter,[6] hurry to my room, or, if it be the day and hour for it, to the church where a congregation is assembled and, as time permits, I say the Ten Commandments, the Creed, and, if I have time, some words of Christ or of Paul, or some psalms, out loud to myself just as a child might do.

It is a good thing to let prayer be the first business of the morning and the last at night.[7] Diligently guard against those false, deluding ideas, which tell you, "Wait a little while. I will pray in an hour; first I must attend to this or that." Such thoughts get you away from prayer into other affairs that so hold your attention and involve you that nothing comes of prayer for that day. This is especially so in emergencies when you have some tasks that seem as good or better than prayer. There is a saying ascribed to St. Jerome:[8] "Everything a believer does is prayer," and a proverb, "He who works faithfully prays twice." This can be said because a believer fears and honors God in his work[9] and remembers the commandment not to wrong anyone, or to try to steal, overcharge, or embezzle. Such thoughts and such faith undoubtedly transform his work into prayer and a sacrifice of praise.

℄ Then again, the contrary must also be true that the work of an unbeliever is outright cursing and so he who works faithlessly

St. Jerome reading in the countryside, by Giovanni Bellini (c. 1430–1516)

7. Luther included morning and evening prayers in his *Small Catechism* (1529) and recommended that the head of each family teach all members of the household to say them daily. In his *German Mass*, 1526 (TAL 3:130–61; LW 53:68–69; WA 19:79–80), Luther called for morning (Matins) and evening or afternoon (Vespers) services on Sunday. Luther also said that in towns where there are schools for boys, each day should begin and end with the singing of some psalms in Latin. This practice appears to be inspired by the recitation of canonical hours in monasteries.

8. St. Jerome (c. 347–420) was one of the foremost theologians of the early Western church. Between 382 and 405 he translated the Old and New Testaments from Hebrew and Greek into Latin, producing the *Vulgata*, which became the standard version of the Bible used in the Roman Catholic Church for centuries. The German critical edition (WA) speculated that Luther had in mind Jerome's commentary on Matt. 25:11, but no passage exactly matches the quote. English translation: St. Jerome, *Commentary on Matthew*, trans. Thomas Scheck, *The Fathers of the Church*, vol. 117 (Washington, DC: Catholic University of America Press, 2008). See also MPL 26:186.

9. For Luther, it is not only the clergy who have a religious vocation. Secular forms of work should also be seen as callings ordained by God. In his *To the Christian Nobility* (1520) Luther says: "A cobbler, a smith, a peasant—each has the work and office of his trade. . . . Further, everyone must benefit and serve every other by means of his own work or office so that in this way

[handwritten marginal notes: "God works by believers", "belief", "believers", "258"]

many kinds of work may be done for the bodily and spiritual welfare of the community" (TAL 1:384; LW 44:130; WA 6:409).

10. For Luther, thoughts and feelings were closely connected and interdependent. For him, "heart" (*Herz*) included both reason and emotions, in contrast to modern parlance, which more commonly associates "heart" solely with emotions. Compare Matt. 24:19: "Out of the heart come evil thoughts." See Birgit Stolt, *Martin Luthers Rhetorik des Herzens* (Tübingen: J. C. B. Mohr/Paul Siebeck, 2000); and idem, "Luther's Faith of 'The Heart': Experience, Emotion, and Reason," in Christine Helmer, ed., *The Global Luther: A Theologian for Modern Times* (Minneapolis: Fortress Press, 2009), 131–50.

11. Luke 11 records the Lord's Prayer and a parable pointing to the importance of persistence in prayer. The quoted verse, however, comes from 1 Thess. 5:17. → *pray w̄ ceasing.*

curses twice. By the thoughts of his heart[10] as well as his work he scorns God. He thinks about violating the commandment and about how to take advantage of his neighbor, to steal and to embezzle. For, what else can such thoughts be but vain curses against God and man, which makes one's work and effort a double curse by which a man also curses himself. In the end such people are beggars and bunglers.) – *not nec. so – wrong*

Christ openly speaks of continual prayer in Luke 11,[11] "Pray without ceasing." One must unceasingly guard against sin and wrongdoing, something one cannot do unless one fears God and keeps his commandment in mind, as Ps. 1[:1, 2] says, "Blessed is he who meditates upon God's law day and night, etc."[i]

Yet we must be careful not to break the habit of true prayer and imagine other works to be necessary which, after all, are nothing of the kind. Thus at the end we become lazy and lax, cold and listless toward prayer. The devil who besets us is not lax nor lazy, and our flesh is all too ready and eager to sin and is averse to the spirit of prayer. Now, when your heart has been warmed by such recitation to yourself [of the Ten Commandments, the words of Christ, etc.] and is intent upon the matter, kneel or stand with your hands folded and your eyes are directed toward heaven and speak out loud or think as briefly as you can:

"O Heavenly Father, dear God, I am a poor unworthy sinner. I do not deserve to raise my eyes or hands toward you or to pray. But because you have commanded us all to pray and have promised to hear us and because you have taught us through your dear Son, Jesus Christ, both how and what to pray, I come to you in obedience to your word, trusting in your gracious promise. I pray in the name of my Lord Jesus Christ together with all your saints and Christians on earth as he has taught me: 'Our Father in heaven . . .'"

---

i   Luther paraphrases the text, making one sentence from parts of two verses.

The Lord's Prayer

The First Petition[12]

Pray through the whole prayer, word for word, then repeat one part or as much as you wish, perhaps the first petition: "Hallowed be your name," and say: "Yes, Lord God, dear Father, hallowed be your name, both in us and throughout the whole world. Destroy and root out the abominations, idolatry, and heresy of the Turk, the pope, and all false teachers and factious spirits[13] who falsely bear your name and thus shamefully abuse it and horribly blaspheme it. They insistently boast that they teach your word and the laws of the church, though they really use the devil's lies and trickery in your name to wretchedly seduce so many poor souls throughout the world, even killing and shedding much innocent blood, and in such persecution they believe that they render you a divine service.

"Dear Lord God, convert and restrain [them]. Convert those who are still to be converted that they with us and we with them may hallow and praise your name, both with true and pure

Praying Hands
by Albrecht Dürer
(1471–1528)

12. Although Luther states in the *Small Catechism* that God's will comes about whether we pray or not, he thought every person should form the habit of commending herself or himself to God each day for protection and help in every need. He taught that all true prayers are answered, though not necessarily at the time or in the manner that the faithful request. They should pray boldly, but God may improve on their petitions. If what they ask for glorifies God's name and honors his kingdom, God hears their prayers (WA TR 1:603 n.1212; LW 54:3–114).

13. The Turks were Muslims and denied the divinity and crucifixion of Christ. During the sixteenth century the Ottoman Turks were also seen as a serious political threat because they repeatedly attempted to conquer central Europe. In 1541, Luther wrote a more specific "Appeal for Prayer against the Turks" (LW 43:213–41; WA 51:585–625). In his later polemics, Luther often expressed his belief that the devil was using the Turks, his Catholic opponents, and the more radical Protestant reformers (the *Rottengeister* or factious spirits) to undermine his reform efforts. See Mark U. Edwards Jr., *Luther's Last Battles: Politics and Polemics 1531–1546* (Minneapolis: Fortress Press, 1983).

doctrine and with a good and holy life. Restrain those who are unwilling to be converted so that they are forced to cease from misusing, defiling, and dishonoring your holy name and from misleading the poor people. Amen."

The Second Petition

"Your kingdom come." Say: "O dear Lord, God and Father, you see how worldly wisdom and reason[14] not only profane your name and ascribe the honor due to you to lies and to the devil, but how they also take the power, might, wealth, and glory which you have given them on earth for ruling the world and thereby serving you, and use it in their own ambition to oppose your kingdom.[15] They are many and mighty, thick, fat, and full; they plague and hinder the tiny flock of your kingdom who are weak, despised, and few. They will not tolerate your flock on earth and think that by plaguing them they render a great and godly service to you. Dear Lord, God and Father, convert [them] and defend [us]. Convert those who are still to become children and members of your kingdom so that they with us and we with them may serve you in your kingdom in right faith and true love and that from your kingdom, which has begun, we may enter into your eternal kingdom. Defend us against those who will not turn away their might and power from the destruction of your kingdom so that when they are cast down from their thrones and humbled, they will have to cease from their efforts. Amen."

The Third Petition

"Your will be done on earth as it is in heaven." Say: "O dear Lord, God and Father, you know that the world, if it cannot destroy your name or exterminate your kingdom, is busy day and night with wicked tricks, carrying out many intrigues and strange attacks, whispering together in secret counsel, giving mutual encouragement and support, threatening and spouting off, going about with every evil intention to destroy your name, word, kingdom, and children.

"Therefore, dear Lord, God and Father, convert [them] and defend [us]. Convert those who have yet to acknowledge your good will that they with us and we with them may obey your will and for your sake readily, patiently, and joyously bear every evil,

---

14. Luther was not opposed to the use of reason in its appropriate domain, i.e., worldly affairs and human relations, but said that regarding divine things and matters of faith "reason is like a blind horse" (WA 10/1:530f.). See B. A. Gerrish, *Grace and Reason: A Study in the Theology of Luther* (Oxford: Clarendon Press, 1962), 25–27.

15. Although Luther thought that secular government was ordained by God, he also noted in *On Temporal Authority* (1523) that "the secular lords, who should rule countries and peoples outwardly, do not do so; instead, the only thing they know how to do is to poll and fleece, heap one tax on another, let loose a bear here, a wolf there. There is no good faith or honesty to be found amongst them." (LW 45:109; WA 11:265).

cross, and adversity, and thereby acknowledge, test, and experience your kind, gracious, and perfect will. But defend us against those who in their rage, fury, hate, threats, and evil desires do not cease to do us harm. Make their wicked schemes, tricks, and devices come to nothing so that these may be turned against them, as we sing in Ps. 7[:15, 16].[16] Amen."

The Fourth Petition

"Give us this day our daily bread." Say: "Dear Lord, God and Father, grant us your blessing also in this temporal and physical life. Graciously grant us blessed peace. Protect us against war and discord.[17] Grant to our dear emperor fortune and success against his enemies. Grant him wisdom and understanding to rule unhindered and prosperously over his earthly kingdom. Grant to all kings, princes, and rulers good counsel and the will to preserve their domains and their subjects in tranquility and justice. Especially aid and guide our dear prince N.,[18] under

16. Ps. 7:15-16: "They make a pit, digging it out, and fall into the hole that they have made. Their mischief returns upon their own heads and on their own heads their violence descends."

17. Germany had experienced a significant amount of discord in the decade before this treatise was written. The German Peasants' Revolt, which took over 100,000 lives, ended in 1525. In 1529, a Turkish army under Suleiman the Magnificent (c. 1494–1566) invaded Hungary once again and besieged Vienna.

18. At the time Luther wrote this piece, his prince was John Frederick the Magnanimous (1503–1554), the elector of Saxony, a strong supporter of his Evangelical reforms. Although Emperor Charles V (1500–1558), at the Diet of Worms, declared Luther an outlaw whom anyone could kill without punishment, Luther continued to pray for his well-being. This fits with what he goes on to say about the fifth petition, concerning forgiveness.

Martin Luther and John Frederick I, elector of Saxony (also known as John the Magnanimous), kneel at the cross of Jesus. John Frederick commissioned the Jena edition of Luther's works, in which this woodcut appears.

19. Luther sometimes spoke of three divinely ordained estates (*Stände*): the priestly office, the family, and the civil government (*Kirche, Haus, Staat,* or *ecclesia, oeconomia, politia*). Here, however, he is referring to the traditional medieval division of society into the nobility, the clergy, and the common people. In the sixteenth century, further distinctions were developing within the last category, between the burgher class, made up of citizens of towns who were members of guilds or worked as merchants, and the peasants, who continued to work the land.

20. Revelation 12:9 says that the devil, "the deceiver of the whole world, was thrown down to the earth, and his angels were thrown down with him." Luther did not speculate often about angels but believed that "the evil angels or devils, who are invisible, are enemies more bitter than our visible foes" (LW 4:256; WA 43:319) and that the good angels are busy with the task of keeping these enemies from doing harm (LW 3:270; WA 43:68f.). For Luther's persistent sense of the devil's influence in the world, see Heiko Oberman, *Luther: Man between God and the Devil,* trans. Eileen Walliser-Schwarzbart (New York: Doubleday/Image Books, 1982).

21. During the Middle Ages, it was deemed important to confess all sins specifically to a priest in order to receive absolution. The church distinguished between mortal sins, which condemned one to hell if not confessed, and venial sins or lesser sins, which incurred a penalty that must be removed through the doing of penance or through a process of purgation after death.

whose protection and shelter you maintain us, so that he may be protected against all harm and reign blessedly, secure from evil tongues and disloyal people. Grant to all his subjects grace to serve him loyally and obediently. Grant to every estate[19]—townsmen or farmers—to be devout and to display charity and loyalty toward each other. Give us favorable weather and good harvest. I commend to you my house and property, wife and child. Grant that I may manage them well, supporting and educating them as a Christian should. Defend us and put a stop to the Destroyer and all his wicked angels[20] who would do us harm and mischief in this life. Amen."

The Fifth Petition[21]

"Forgive us our sin as we forgive those who sin against us."[j] Say: "O dear Lord, God and Father, enter not into judgment against us because no man living is righteous before you. Do not count it against us as a sin that we are so unthankful for your ineffable goodness, spiritual and physical, or that we stumble and sin many times every day, more often than we can know or recognize, Ps. 19[:12].[k] Do not look upon how good or how wicked we are but only upon the infinite compassion that you have bestowed upon us in Christ, your dear Son. Grant forgiveness also to those who have harmed or wronged us, as we forgive them from our hearts. They inflict the greatest injury upon themselves by arousing your anger in their actions toward us. We are not helped by their ruin; we would much rather that they be saved with us. Amen." (Anyone who feels unable to forgive, let him ask for grace so that he can forgive; but that belongs in a sermon.)

The Sixth Petition

"And lead us not into temptation." Say: "O dear Lord, Father and God, keep us bold and alert, passionate and eager in your word and service, so that we do not become complacent, lazy, and sluggish as though we had already achieved everything. In that way

---

j   Luther uses the German word *Schuld* in the singular. It can be translated as "sin," "debt," "trespass," or "guilt."

k   Ps. 19:12: "Who can detect their errors? Clear me from hidden faults." (German Bibles list this as v. 13.)

the fierce devil cannot beguile us, surprise us, and deprive us of your precious word or stir up strife and factions among us and lead us into other sin and disgrace, both spiritually and physically. Rather grant us wisdom and strength through your spirit that we may valiantly resist him and gain the victory. Amen."

The Seventh Petition

"But deliver us from evil." Say: "O dear Lord, God and Father, this wretched life is so full of misery, misfortune, and uncertainty, so full of faithlessness and malice (as St. Paul says, "The days are evil" [Eph. 5:16])*l* that we might easily grow weary of life and long for death. But you, dear Father, know our frailty; therefore help us to pass in safety through so much wickedness and villainy; and, when our time comes, in your mercy grant us a gracious final hour and a blessed departure from this vale of sorrows so that in the face of death we do not become fearful or despondent but in firm faith commit our souls into your hands. Amen."

Finally, mark this, that you must always speak the "Amen" firmly. Never doubt that God in his mercy will surely hear you and say "yes" to your prayers. Never think that you are kneeling or standing alone, rather think that the whole of Christendom, all devout Christians, are standing there beside you and you are standing among them in a common, united petition which God cannot disdain. Do not leave your prayer without having said or thought, "Very well, God has heard my prayer; this I know as a certainty and a truth." That is what Amen means.

You should also know that I do not want you to recite all these words in your prayer. That would make it nothing but mere chatter and idle prattle, read word for word out of a book as were the rosaries by the laity and the prayers of the clerics and monks.[22] Rather do I want your heart to be stirred and guided concerning the thoughts that ought to be comprehended in the Lord's Prayer. These thoughts may be expressed, if your heart is rightly warmed and inclined toward prayer, in many different ways and with more words or fewer. I do not bind myself to such words or syllables, but say my prayers in one fashion today,

Luther, however, did not think of sin as specific sinful acts. Instead, he viewed sin more as a general condition of being turned away from God toward one's self (*incurvatus in se*). Citing Rom. 14:23, Luther held that all human acts are sinful until faith restores the relationship with God. See Matt Jenson, *Gravity of Sin: Augustine, Luther, and Barth on homo incurvatus in se* (New York: T&T Clark, 2006).

22. A rosary (from Latin for "garland of roses") is a string of prayer beads. The Dominican Order encouraged people to repeat sets of ten Hail Mary prayers preceded by one recitation of the Lord's Prayer. During the fifteenth century, a German monk introduced the practice of pausing to meditate on a theme after each decade of prayers, but the common people used rosaries more simply to keep track of how many prayers they had said. The German word *Pfaffen*, translated here as "clerics," refers to any individual who has received the clerical tonsure, including bishops, priests, deacons, and subdeacons. Each day, clerics were supposed to recite a set of prayers known as the Divine Office.

---

l   Eph. 5:16: "Be careful how you live . . . making the most of the time because the days are evil."

23. Luther quotes twice in this text from one of the books of the Apocrypha, the Wisdom of Jesus ben Sirach, also known as Ecclesiasticus. Although Luther did not consider the Apocrypha to be as inspired as the Old and New Testament, he translated it into German and continued to include its books in the complete Bible he published in 1534. Luther's version of Sirach 18:23 is close to the Latin Vulgate, but most modern translations, working from different manuscripts, render the verse quite differently: "Before making a vow, prepare yourself."

24. Luther imagines the priest fulfilling the daily requirement of reciting prayers from a breviary while simultaneously attending to other mundane tasks. The first two Latin phrases are from Psalm 69, which was repeated several times a day at the start of the liturgy of the hours: "Be pleased O God to deliver me" and "Make haste to help me." The third sentence completes the opening lines of the liturgy: "Glory be to the Father, and to the Son, and to the Holy Spirit."

25. In a lecture on Gen. 17:19-22, Luther said: "To pray is not to recite a number of psalms or to roar in churches, as monks usually do, but to have serious thoughts by which the soul establishes a fellowship between him who prays and Him who hears the prayer" (WA 42:662; LW 3:160).

26. The term "canonical hours" is a synonym for the Divine Office, which consisted of psalms, prayers, and lessons publicly chanted in churches or oratories at various times throughout the day. From as early as the fifth century, priests and clerics were expected to recite the hours in private

in another tomorrow, depending upon my mood and feeling. I stay however, as nearly as I can, with the same general thoughts and ideas. It may happen occasionally that I may wander among so many ideas in one petition that I forgo the other six. If such an abundance of good thoughts comes to us we ought to disregard the other petitions, make room for such thoughts, listen in silence, and under no circumstances obstruct them. The Holy Spirit himself preaches here, and one word of his sermon is far better than a thousand of our prayers. Many times I have learned more from one prayer than I might have learned from much reading and speculation.

It is of great importance that the heart be made ready and eager for prayer. As the Preacher says, "Prepare your heart for prayer, and do not tempt God" [Ecclus. 18:23].[23] What else is it but tempting God when your mouth babbles and the heart is distracted? Like the priest who prayed, *"Deus in adjutorium meum intende.* Farmhand, did you unhitch the horses? *Domine ad adjuvandum me festina.* Maid, go out and milk the cow. *Gloria patri et filio et spiritui sancto.*[24] Run, boy. I wish the fever would take you!"[m] I have heard many such prayers in my experience under the papacy; almost all of their prayers are of this sort.[25] This is making a mockery of God and it would be better to admit they are making a game of it if they cannot or do not care to do better. In my day I have prayed many such canonical hours[26] myself, regrettably, and in such a manner that the psalm or the allotted time came to an end before I even realized whether I was at the beginning or in the middle.

Though not all of them blurt out the words as did the above-mentioned cleric and mix business and prayer, they do it by the thoughts in their hearts. They jump from one thing to another[27] in their thoughts and when it is all over they do not know what

m   The word translated here as "fever" is *Ritt* in German. It refers to a malaria-like illness characterized by regular intervals of fever and chills.

Das Schlaraffenland (*The Fool's Paradise*)
by Pieter Bruegel the Elder, 1567

they have done or what they talked about. They start with *Laudate*[n] and right away they are in a fool's paradise.[28] It seems to me that if someone could see what arises as prayer from a cold and inattentive heart he would conclude that he had never seen a more ridiculous juggling game.[o] But, praise God, it is now clear to me that a person who forgets what he has said has not prayed well. In a good prayer one fully remembers every word and thought from the beginning to the end of the prayer.

It is just like a good and attentive barber who keeps his thoughts, attention, and eyes on the razor and the hair and does not forget how far he has gotten with his shaving or cutting.[29]

---

n   Here *Laudate* ("Praise the Lord") refers to Psalms 148, 149, and 150, which were sung together as one psalm in the canonical hours, especially for Lauds, or Morning Prayer.

o   In German, a *Gaukler* is a juggler, so *Gaukelspiel* could be translated as "juggling game."

when they could not assist at the public Office. It was considered a serious sin to neglect the hours. When Luther was a monk, he was sometimes so busy with his various daily duties that he fell weeks behind in the required recitation of the Divine Office. Since he took this duty seriously, he would sometimes shut himself up in his cell on weekends without any food or drink and repeatedly read the required texts until he was caught up. See Martin Brecht, *Martin Luther: His Road to Reformation 1483–1521*, trans. James L. Schaaf (Philadelphia: Fortress Press, 1985), 64–65.

27. Luther uses the unusual phrase *"werfen das Hunderste in's Tausendste"* ("throw the hundredth into the thousandth"). This phrase is a reference to calculations being made for currency exchanges. If a moneychanger did not pay close attention, he could record hundreds as thousands. The phrase came to be a way of talking about "getting carried away."

28. Luther uses the term *Schlaraffenland* in reference to a mythical land of plenty. In Middle High German, *schluraff* is a term for a lazy oaf. Sebastian Brant (1457–1521), the humanist social critic from Strassburg, wrote about this mythical land in chapter 108 of *The Ship of Fools* (1494), and Hans Sach wrote a poem, *Schlaweraffen Landt*, in 1530. See Scott Horton's translation, "Hans Sach's Schlaraffenland" in *Harper's Magazine*, July 20, 2008. Compare the medieval French myth of the *pays de cocaigne*, carried over into English literature as "the land of Cockaigne."

29. Sixteenth-century barbers cut hair, gave shaves with a straight razor, and also performed minor medical and dental procedures. On barber-surgeons, see Robert Jütte, "A Seventeenth-Century German Barber-Surgeon and His Patients," in *Medical History* 33 (1989): 184–98.

Etching of a barber,
Frankfurt on Main, 1568

30. This hexameter appears frequently in texts from several regions of Europe. The rhyme between *intentus* and *sensus* suggests that it is medieval in origin.

31. Usually Luther calls the prayer *Der Vater Unser* ("The Our Father"), but in this section he uses the Latin equivalent, *Pater Noster*.

If he engages in lots of conversation at the same time or lets his mind wander or look somewhere else he is likely to cut his customer's mouth, nose, or even his throat. Thus if anything is to be done well, it requires the full attention of all one's senses and members, as the proverb says, *"Pluribus intentus, minor est ad singula sensus"*—"A person engaged in multiple pursuits, minds none of them well."[30] How much more does prayer call for concentration and singleness of heart if it is to be a good prayer!

This in short is the way I use the Lord's Prayer when I pray it. To this day I suckle at the Lord's Prayer[31] like a child, and as an old man eat and drink from it and never get my fill. It is the very best prayer, even better than the psalter, which is so very dear to me. It is surely evident that a real master composed and taught it.

What a great shame[p] that the prayer of such a master is prattled and chattered so irreverently all over the world! How many pray the Lord's Prayer several thousand times in the course of a year, and if they were to keep on doing so for a thousand years they would not have tasted nor prayed one letter or one stroke of a letter of it![32] In a word, the Lord's Prayer is the greatest martyr on earth (along with the name and word of God). Everybody tortures and abuses it; few take comfort and joy in its proper use.

The Ten Commandments[33]

If I have time and opportunity to go through the Lord's Prayer, I do the same with the Ten Commandments. I take one part after another and free myself as much as possible from distractions in order to pray. I divide each commandment into four parts, thereby fashioning a garland of four entwined strands. That is, I think of each commandment as, first, instruction, which is really what it is intended to be, and consider what the Lord God so earnestly demands of me. Second, I turn it into a thanksgiving; third, a confession; and fourth, a prayer. I do so in thoughts or words such as these:

The First Commandment

"I am the Lord your God, etc. You are to have no other gods besides me, etc." Here I first consider that God expects and teaches me to trust him sincerely in all things. It is his most earnest intention to be my God, so I must think of him in this way at the risk of losing eternal salvation. My heart must not build upon anything else or trust in any other thing, be it wealth, prestige, wisdom, might, holiness, or any other creature. Second, I give thanks for God's infinite compassion by which he has come to me, a lost mortal, in such a fatherly way and, without my asking, seeking, or deserving him, has offered to be my God, to care for me, and to be my comfort, protection, help, and strength in every time of need. We poor blind mortals have sought so many gods and would have to seek them still if he did not enable us to hear him

32. Luther may have in mind the many recitations of the Lord's Prayer that were done in his day to complete the penance assigned by priests in the Sacrament of Confession. Although the rosary could be a sophisticated aid to devotion, combining prayer and meditation, many who used it simply counted their beads and rushed through the numerous repetitions of the Lord's Prayer and the Hail Mary prayer.

33. In this treatise, as in his other writings on prayer, Luther looks to a text for instruction and that, in turn, inspires his prayers. He combines catechesis and prayer. For Luther, distinguishing between law and gospel was an essential starting point for the study of Scripture. He always looks first to the law and then to the gospel. The law (as seen in the Ten Commandments) teaches people that they are sick and cannot measure up to what they should do. The gospel (as described in the Creed) shows the sick person where to get the medicine—grace—that restores health. See the preface to his *Little Prayer Book*, pp. 165–67 in this volume.

p   Luther uses the phrase "*Jammer über Jammer*" ("sorrow above [all] sorrow[s]"). *Es ist ein Jammer* means "It is such a shame."

openly tell us in our own language that he wants to be our God. How could we ever—in all eternity—thank God enough! Third, I confess and acknowledge my great sin and ingratitude for having so shamefully despised such a sublime teaching and precious gift throughout my whole life, and for having horridly provoked his wrath by countless acts of idolatry. I repent of these and ask for his grace. Fourth, I pray and say: "O my God and Lord, help me by your grace to learn and understand your commandments more fully every day and to live by them in sincere confidence. Preserve my heart so that I shall never again become forgetful and ungrateful, that I may never seek after other gods or other consolation on earth or in any creature, but cling truly and solely to you, my only God. Amen, dear Lord God and Father. Amen."

The Second Commandment

Afterward, if time and inclination permit, the Second Commandment likewise in four strands, in this way: "You are not to take the name of the Lord your God in vain," etc. First, I learn that I should regard God's name as honorable, holy, and beautiful. I should not swear, curse, lie, be boastful, nor seek honor and repute for myself, but instead I should humbly invoke his name, pray, adore, praise, and extol it. I should let it be all my honor and glory that he is my God and that I am his lowly creature and unworthy servant.

Second, I give thanks to him for these precious gifts, that he has revealed and imparted his name to me, that I can glory in his name and be called God's servant and creature, etc., that his name is my refuge like a mighty fortress to which the righteous man can flee and find protection, as Solomon says [Prov. 18:10].[9]

Third, I confess and acknowledge that I have grievously and shamefully sinned against this commandment all my life. I have not only failed to invoke, extol, and honor his holy name, but have also been ungrateful for such gifts and have, by swearing, lying, and betraying, misused them in the pursuit of shame and sin. This I regret and ask grace and forgiveness, etc.

Fourth, I ask for help and strength henceforth to learn [to obey] this commandment and to be preserved from such evil

---

9   Prov. 18:10: "The name of the LORD is a strong tower [*eine feste Burg*]; the righteous run into it and are safe."

ingratitude, abuse, and sin against his holy name, and that I may be found grateful in revering and honoring his name. I repeat here what I previously said in reference to the Lord's Prayer: if in the midst of such thoughts the Holy Spirit begins to preach in your heart with rich, enlightening thoughts, honor him by letting go of these prepared thoughts; be still and listen to him who can do better than you can. Remember what he says and note it well and you will behold wondrous things in the law of God, as David says [Ps. 119:18].[r]

The Third Commandment

"You are to sanctify the day of rest."[34] I learn from this, first of all, that the day of rest has not been instituted for the sake of being idle or indulging in worldly pleasures, but in order that we may observe it respectfully. However, it is not sanctified by our works and actions—since our works are not holy—but by the word of God, which alone is wholly pure and sacred and which sanctifies everything that comes in contact with it, be it time, place, person, labor, rest, etc. For through the word our works are also sanctified. As St. Paul says in 1 Tim. 4[:5], "Every creature is sanctified by the word and prayer." I realize therefore that on the day of rest I must, above all, hear and contemplate God's word. Thereafter I should give thanks in my own words, praise God for all his benefits, and pray for myself and for the whole world. He who so conducts himself on the day of rest sanctifies it. He who fails to do so is worse than the person who works on the day of rest.

Second, I thank God in this commandment for the great and beautiful goodness and grace which he has given us through his word and preaching. And he has instructed us to make use of it, especially on the day of rest, for meditation by the human heart can never exhaust such a treasure. His word is the only light in the darkness of this life, a word of life, consolation, and supreme blessedness. Where this precious and saving word is absent, nothing remains but empty and terrifying darkness, error and factions, death and every calamity, and the devil's own tyranny, as we can see with our own eyes every day.

34. The Third Commandment concerns the Sabbath, celebrated as a day of rest by Jews from Friday sundown to Saturday sundown. Very early on, the Christian movement switched to observing Sunday as a special day for worship, in commemoration of the resurrection of Christ on the first day of the week. Luther uses a broader word, *Feiertag*, in this section, meaning a holy day or a day of religious celebration. In recent times, the word in German has come to refer more commonly to any kind of holiday.

[handwritten: Luther speaking. The word says is is a day of rest]

r   Ps. 119:18: "Open my eyes, so that I may behold wondrous things out of your law."

35. Luther was concerned throughout his career with the danger of divisions or schisms within the Christian community. He made clear in his own reform efforts that he was not seeking to create a new church. In 1521 he came out of hiding at the Wartburg to address the confusion created by his university colleague Andreas Karlstadt (c. 1480–1541) and the "prophets" from Zwickau who attempted to introduce radical reforms in worship practices. In his *Invocavit Sermons* of 1522, Luther suggested that reform efforts should be carefully paced and that persuasion rather than force should be used to bring about change. In the same year he wrote a treatise against insurrection and another about the extent to which temporal authorities should be obeyed (see LW 45:51–129; TAL 5, forthcoming). Around the time Luther was writing this work, a new group of "factious spirits" had arisen in Germany. In 1534 Anabaptist radicals took over the city of Münster in Westphalia and renamed it "The New Jerusalem." They exiled many opponents and forcibly baptized others.

36. The barber who prompted Luther to write this piece once proposed himself to write a book warning people about the power of the devil. In response, Luther wrote a humorous poem about this which included the lines:

> So brash and bold the devil is—
> Full of knavery, trick, and guile,
> That Master Peter had better look
>   sharp
> Lest he try to trick the devil
> And it backfires on himself . . .

(LW 52:357–59; Walch, *Dr. Martin Luthers sämmtliche Schriften*, 9:1821–24).

Third, I confess and acknowledge great sin and wicked ingratitude on my part because all my life I have made disgraceful use of the day of rest and have thereby despised his precious and dear word so miserably. I have been too lazy, listless, and tired of the word to listen to it, let alone to have desired it sincerely or to have been grateful for it. I have let my dear God proclaim his word to me in vain, have abandoned the noble treasure, and have trampled it underfoot. He has tolerated this in his great and divine mercy and has not ceased in his fatherly, divine love and faithfulness to keep on preaching to me and calling me to the salvation of my soul. For this I repent and ask for grace and forgiveness.

Fourth, I pray for myself and for the whole world that the gracious Father may preserve us in his holy word and not withdraw it from us because of our sin, ingratitude, and laziness. May he preserve us from factious spirits and false teachers,[35] and may he send faithful and honest laborers into his harvest,[s] that is, devout pastors and preachers. May he grant us grace humbly to hear, accept, and honor their words as his own words and to offer our sincere thanks and praise.

The Fourth Commandment

"You are to honor your father and your mother." First, I learn here to acknowledge God, my Creator; how wondrously he has created me, body and soul; and how he has given me life through my parents and has instilled in them the desire to care for me, the fruit of their bodies, with all their power. He has brought me into this world, has sustained and cared for me, nurtured and educated me with great diligence, carefulness, and concern, through danger, trouble, and work. Up to this very hour he has protected me, his creature, and helped me in countless dangers and troubles. It is as though he were creating me anew every moment. But the devil does not willingly concede us one single moment of life.[36]

Second, I thank the rich and gracious Creator on behalf of myself and all the world that he has established and assured in this commandment the increase and preservation of the human

---

s　Matt. 9:38: "Ask the Lord of the harvest to send out laborers into his harvest."

race, that is, of households and of states.[t] Without these two institutions or governments the world could not stand a single year, because without government there can be no peace, and where there is no peace there can be no family;[u] without family, children cannot be begotten or raised, and fatherhood and motherhood would cease to be. It is the purpose of this commandment to guard and preserve both family and state, to admonish children and subjects to be obedient. This must happen and, if it does not, he will let no violation go unpunished—otherwise children would have torn the household apart long ago by their disobedience, and subjects would have laid waste to the state through rebellion, because they outnumber parents and rulers.

Third, I confess and acknowledge my wicked disobedience and sin; in defiance of God's commandment I have not honored or obeyed my parents; I have often provoked and offended them, have been impatient with their parental discipline, have grumbled about and scorned their

Knight, Death, and the Devil
by Albrecht Dürer, 1513

loving admonition and have preferred to go along with loose company and evil companions. God afflicts such disobedient children and withholds from them a long life; many of them succumb and perish in disgrace before they reach adulthood. Whoever does not obey father and mother must obey the executioner

---

t   Luther uses the German terms *Haus- und Stadtwesen* and then repeats the terms in Latin: *oeconomiam und politiam*.

u   The German term is *Hauswesen*, which can also be translated as "household" or "home."

37. Luther attributes weighty responsibilities to parents. They should not only prepare their children for a successful life in secular society but should also attend to their spiritual training. In his comments on the Fourth Commandment in the *Large Catechism*, Luther states that if they neglect this duty they are at risk of losing divine grace. In turn, since children owe so much to their parents they should view them as God's representatives and accord to them both love and honor. Other superiors such as the schoolmaster and those in positions of civil authority are also owed obedience because their roles are, in a sense, an extension of "fatherhood"; BC, 400–410.

38. Luther may be thinking of 1 Tim. 2:1-4: "First of all, then, I urge that supplications, prayers, intercessions, and thanksgivings be made for everyone, for kings and all who are in high positions, so that we may lead a quiet and peaceable life in all godliness and dignity."

or otherwise come, through God's wrath, to an evil end, etc. Of all this I repent and ask for grace and forgiveness.

Fourth, I pray for myself and for all the world that God would bestow his grace and pour his blessing richly upon the family and the state, so that from this time on we may be devout, honor our parents, obey our superiors, and resist the devil when he entices us to be disobedient and rebellious. Grant that we may help improve home and nation by our actions and thus preserve the peace, all to the praise and glory of God for our own benefit and for the prosperity of all. Grant that we may acknowledge these his gifts and be thankful for them.

At this point we should add a prayer for our parents and superiors, that God may grant them understanding and wisdom to govern and rule us in peace and happiness.[37] May he preserve them from tyranny, from riot and fury, and turn them from such things so that they honor God's word and do not persecute or do injustice to anyone. Such excellent gifts must be sought by prayer, as St. Paul teaches;[38] otherwise the devil will reign in the palace and everything will fall into chaos and confusion.

If you are a father or mother, you should at this point remember your children and the other members of your household.[v]

Scene from a book on prayers before meals
by Johann Hoffer (1534–1583)

---

v   The German term is *Gesinde*, which can also be translated as "servants."

Pray earnestly to the dear Father, who has set you in an office of honor in his name and intends that you also be honored by the name "father." Ask that he grant you grace and blessing to look after and support your wife, children, and workers in a godly and Christian manner. May he give you wisdom and strength to train them well and give them a heart and will to follow your instruction and be obedient. Both your children and the way they develop are God's gifts, both that they turn out well and that they remain so. Otherwise the home is nothing but a pigsty and school for rascals, as one can see among the uncouth and godless people.

The Fifth Commandment

"You are not to kill." Here I learn, first of all, that God desires me to love my neighbor, so that I do him no bodily harm, either by word or action, neither injure nor take revenge upon him in anger, vexation, envy, hatred, or for any evil reason. I should realize that I am obliged to assist and counsel him in every bodily need. In this commandment God commands me to protect my neighbor's body and in turn commands my neighbor to protect my own. As Sirach says, "He has committed to each of us his neighbor."[w]

Second, I give thanks for such ineffable love, care, and faithfulness toward me by which he has placed such a strong protection and wall around my body. All are obliged to look after what is mine and protect me, and I, in turn, must behave likewise toward all others. He upholds this command and, where it is not observed, he has established the sword as punishment for those who do not live up to it. Were it not for this excellent commandment and ordinance, the devil would instigate such a massacre among men that no one could live in safety for a single hour— as happens when God becomes angry and inflicts punishment upon a disobedient and ungrateful world.

w   The German critical edition connects this phrase to Ecclus. 9:21. In Luther's 1534 Bible that verse reads, "*Erlerne mit allen vleis deinen nehesten*" ("Learn from [learn to know] your neighbor"). The American edition of Luther's Works (LW) suggests that Luther is referring to Ecclus. 9:14. In Luther's Bible this verse says, "*Übergibt einen alten Freund nicht auf*" ("Do not forsake an old friend"). See also Ecclus. 29:20: "Help your neighbor as much as you can"; and Ecclus. 22:23: "Stand by [your neighbor] when he is in trouble."

39. More literally, "in the heart."
Here again, Luther refers to the heart,
whereas modern references might be
to the "mind" and its "thoughts."
See n. 10, p. 258.

Third, I confess and lament my own wickedness and that of the world, not only that we are so terribly ungrateful for such fatherly love and care toward us—but what is especially scandalous, that we do not acknowledge this commandment and teaching, are unwilling to learn it, and neglect it as though it did not concern us or we had no part in it. We amble along complacently, feeling no remorse that, in defiance of this commandment, we despise our neighbors,[x] desert them, persecute, injure, or even kill them in our thoughts.[39] We indulge in anger, rage, and villainy as though we were doing a fine and noble thing. Really, it is high time that we started to deplore and bewail[y] how much we have acted like rogues and like blind, wild, and unfeeling people who tread on, kick, scratch, tear, bite, and devour one another like furious beasts and pay no heed to this serious command of God, etc.

Fourth, I pray the dear Father to lead us to an understanding of this his sacred commandment and to help us keep it and live in accordance with it. May God preserve us from the murderer who is the master of every form of murder and violence. May God grant us his rich grace that we and all others may treat each other in kindly, gentle, and generous ways, forgiving one another from the heart, bearing each other's faults and shortcomings in a Christian and brotherly manner, and thus living together in true peace and unity, as the commandment teaches and requires us to do.

The Sixth Commandment

"You shall not commit adultery." Here I learn once more what God intends and expects me to do, namely, to live chastely, decently, and temperately, both in thoughts and in words and actions, and not to disgrace any man's wife, daughter, or maidservant. More than this, I ought to assist, save, protect, and do everything that serves to uphold their honor and discipline; I should also help to silence the idle loudmouths who want to steal or strip them of their honor. All this I am obliged to do, and God expects me not only to leave my neighbor's wife and family

---

x   This term and the pronouns following are singular in the original.

y   Most literally, "It is bewailing and crying time" (*Hie ist's Klagens und Schreiens Zeit*).

unmolested, but also to uphold and protect his good character and honor, just as I would want my neighbor to do for me and mine in keeping with this commandment.

Second, I thank my faithful and dear Father for his grace and benevolence by which he takes my husband, son, servant, wife, daughter, maidservant into his care and protection and forbids so sternly and firmly anything that would bring them into disrepute. God gives me a safe escort by this commandment and does not let violations go unpunished, even if he himself has to act where someone disregards and violates the commandment and precept. No one escapes; he must either pay the penalty here and now or eventually atone for such lust in the fires of hell. God desires chastity and will not tolerate adultery. That can be seen every day when the impenitent and profligate are finally overtaken by the wrath of God and perish miserably. Otherwise it would be impossible to guard one's wife, child, and servants against the filthy devil for a single hour or preserve them in honor and decency. There would be unbridled immorality[z] and beastliness all over, as happens when God in his wrath withdraws his hand and permits everything to go to wrack and ruin.

Third, I confess and acknowledge my sin, my own and that of all the world, how I have sinned against this commandment my whole life in thought, word, and action. Not only have I been ungrateful for this excellent teaching and gift, but I have murmured against God for commanding such decency and chastity and not permitting all sorts of fornication and rascality to go unchecked and unpunished. God will not allow marriage to be despised, ridiculed, or condemned, etc. Sins against this commandment are, above all others, the grossest and most conspicuous and cannot be covered up or disguised. For this I am sorry, etc.

Fourth, I pray for myself and all the world that God may grant us grace to keep this commandment gladly and cheerfully in order that we might ourselves live in chastity and also help and support others to do likewise.

Then I continue with the other commandments as I have time or opportunity or am in the mood for it. As I have said before, I do not want anyone to feel bound by my words or thoughts.

---

z   Luther uses the colorful term *Hundehochzeiten* ("dog's wedding"), having in mind the unrestrained sexual instincts of animals.

I only want to offer an example for those who may wish to follow it; let anyone improve it who is able to do so and let him meditate either upon all commandments at one time or on as many as he may desire. For the soul, once it is seriously occupied with a matter, be it good or evil, can ponder more in one moment than the tongue can recite in ten hours or the pen write in ten days. There is something quick, subtle, and mighty about the soul or spirit. It is able to review the Ten Commandments in their fourfold aspect[40] very rapidly if it wants to do so and is in earnest.

The Seventh Commandment

"You shall not steal." First, I can learn here that I must not take my neighbor's property from him or possess it against his will, either in secret or openly. I must not be false or dishonest in any transactions, service, or work, nor profit by fraud, but must support myself by the sweat of my brow[a] and eat my bread in honor. Furthermore, I must see to it that in any of the above-named ways my neighbor is not defrauded, just as I wish for myself. I also learn in this commandment that God, in his fatherly solicitude, protects my possessions and solemnly prohibits anyone to steal from me. Where that is ignored, he has imposed a penalty and has placed the gallows and the rope in the hands of Master Jack the hangman.[b] Where that cannot be done, God metes out punishment and they become beggars in the end, as the proverb says, "Who steals in his youth, goes begging in old age." Likewise, "There is no profit in deceit," or "Unjust gain will not remain."[41]

Second, I give thanks for his steadfast goodness in that he has given such excellent teachings, as well as assurance, and protection to me and to all the world. If it were not for his protection, not a penny or a crumb of bread would be left in the house.

Third, I confess my sins and ingratitude in such instances where I have wronged, cheated, or been false to anyone in my life.

Fourth, I ask that God grant to me and all the world grace to learn from this commandment, to ponder it, and to become better people, so that there may be less theft, robbery, mistreatment, cheating, and injustice and that the Judgment Day, for which all

40. "These are the Ten Commandments in their fourfold aspect, namely, as a little book of instruction, a book of thanksgiving, a penitential book, and a prayer book" (see p. 277 below).

41. The last proverb is a rhyme: "*Übel gewonnen, böslich zerronnen*" (literally, "What has been gained wrongly melts away"). Today, there is a similar German saying, "*Wie gewonnen, so zerronnen*," which is comparable to the English proverb "Easy come, easy go." A proverb of this sort exists in all of the major European languages. A Latin equivalent, "*Mala parta male dilabuntur*," is mentioned in the writings of the Roman orator Cicero (*Orationes Philippicae II*, 27, 65). The Latin version also appears in Erasmus's *Adages* (*Adagiorum chiliades quatuor*) 1, 7, 82.

a   Luther's phrase "*Schweiß meiner Nase*" would more literally be translated as "the sweat of my nose."

b   The proverbial "Jack the hangman" is *Meister Hans* in German.

saints and the whole creation pray, Romans 8[:20-23], shall soon bring this to an end. Amen.

The Eighth Commandment

"You are not to bear false witness." This teaches us, first of all, to be truthful to each other, to shun lies and calumnies, to be glad to speak well of each other, and to delight in hearing what is good about others. Thus a wall has been built around our good reputation and integrity to protect it against malicious loud-mouths and false tongues; God will not let that go unpunished, as was said in the other commandments. We owe God thanks both for the teachings and the protection which he has graciously provided for us.

Third, we confess and ask forgiveness for having spent our lives in ingratitude and sin and having maligned our neighbors^c with false and wicked talk, though we owe them the same preservation of honor and integrity which we desire for ourselves.

Fourth, we ask for help to keep the commandment from now on and to have a wholesome tongue, etc.

The Ninth and Tenth Commandments

"You are not to covet your neighbor's house." Similarly, "his wife," etc. This teaches us first that we shall not dispossess our neighbor of his goods under pretense of legal claims, or reduce, divert, or extort what is his, but help him to keep what is his, just as we wish to be done for ourselves. It is also a protection against the subtleties and chicaneries of shrewd manipulators who will receive their punishment in the end.

Second, we should render thanks to him.

Third, we should repentantly and sorrowfully confess our sins.

Fourth, we should ask for help and strength to become devout and to keep this commandment of God.

These are the Ten Commandments in their fourfold aspect, namely, as a little book of instruction, a book of thanksgiving, a penitential book, and a prayer book. They are intended to help the heart come to itself and to be warmed up to pray. Take

c   Singular in the German.

care, however, not to undertake all of this or so much that one becomes weary in spirit. Likewise, a good prayer should not be lengthy or drawn out, but frequent and ardent. It is enough to consider one section or half a section which kindles a fire in the heart. This the Spirit will grant us and continually instruct us in when, by God's word, our hearts have been cleared and freed of outside thoughts and concerns.

Nothing can be said here about the part of faith and Holy Scriptures [in prayer] because there would be no end to what could be said.[42] With practice one can take the Ten Commandments on one day, a psalm or chapter of Holy Scripture the next day, and use them to kindle a flame in the heart.[d]

A Simple Exercise for Contemplating the Creed

If you have more time, or the inclination, you may treat the Creed in the same manner and make it, too, into a garland of four strands. The Creed, however, consists of three main parts or articles, corresponding to the three Persons of the Divine Majesty, as it has also been previously divided in the Catechism.[43]

The First Article of Creation

"I believe in God the Father almighty, Creator of heaven and earth." Here, first of all, a great light shines into your heart if you permit it to and teaches you in a few words what all the languages of the world and a multitude of books cannot encompass or grasp in words, namely, who you are, whence you came, whence came heaven and earth. You are God's creation, his handiwork, his workmanship. That is, of yourself and in yourself you are nothing, can do nothing, know nothing, are capable of nothing. What were you a thousand years ago? What were heaven and earth six thousand years ago?[44] Nothing, just as that which will never be created is nothing. But what you are, know, can do, and can achieve is God's creation, as you confess [in the

42. Luther does not refer specifically to the psalms in this treatise, but he recommends eight of them in his *Little Prayer Book* (pp. 159–99 in this volume). He used the psalter for his own prayers throughout his life and said that one can find words for any situation in the psalms (LW 35:256).

In his commentaries and sermons as well as in his treatises on prayer, Luther also drew attention to many examples of prayer that are found in the Bible. For more on that, see Mary Jane Haemig, "Praying amidst Life's Perils: How Luther Used Biblical Examples to Teach Prayer," *Seminary Ridge Review* 13, no. 2 (Spring 2011): 25–40.

43. Luther placed the Apostles' Creed second, after the Ten Commandments and before the Lord's Prayer, in his *Small Catechism* and *Large Catechism*. Medieval catechisms usually divided the Creed into twelve parts. In contrast, Luther understands the Creed as having three parts corresponding to the three persons of the Trinity.

44. In his lectures on Genesis, Luther also stated: "We know from Moses that the world was not in existence before 6,000 years ago" (LW 1:3; WA 42:3).

---

d   The first edition of this writing ends here. Later editions went on to use the three articles of the Creed as the starting point for further prayers.

Creed] by your own mouth. Therefore you have nothing to boast of before God except that you are nothing and he is your Creator who can annihilate you at any moment. Reason knows nothing of such a light. Many great people have sought to know what heaven and earth, humans and creatures are and have found no answer. But here it is declared and faith affirms that God has created everything out of nothing. Here is the soul's garden of pleasure,[45] in which we can stroll, enjoying the works of God—but it would take too long to describe all that.

Second, we should here give thanks to God that in his kindness he has created us out of nothing and provides for our daily needs out of nothing—has made us to be creatures with body and soul, intelligence, and five senses, who are ordained to be masters of earth, of fish, bird, and beast, etc. On this, hear Genesis, chapters one to three.

Third, we should confess and lament our lack of faith and gratitude in failing to take this to heart, or to believe, ponder, and acknowledge it. We are worse than unthinking beasts.

Fourth, we pray for a true and confident faith that sincerely esteems and trusts God to be our Creator, as this article declares.

Page from a copy
of *Hortulus animae*,
first published in 1498

45. The phrase Luther uses here, *Seelen Lustgarten*, would have been familiar to many readers as the title of a popular Catholic prayer book first printed in Strassburg in 1498. *The Pleasure Garden of the Soul*, or *Hortulus animae* in Latin, was the German counterpart to the devotional book known in France and England as the *Book of Hours*. It contained a variety of prayers but at its center was a liturgical devotion known as the Hours of Our Lady. Luther's advice on prayer, however, is notable for the absence of any prayers addressed to Mary or the saints. He thought the *Hortulus animae* needed a thorough reform because "it gave rise to countless false beliefs" (LW 43:11f.). The image of a pleasure garden also reinforces Luther's advice that one should set aside time to pray in a relaxed but focused manner, strolling through the thoughts inspired by the words of the Creed about creation and redemption, rather than rushing through prayers out of habit or repeating them superficially just because one is expected to perform such acts of piety.

The Second Article of Redemption

"And in Jesus Christ, his only Son, our Lord," etc. Again a great light shines forth and teaches us how Christ, God's Son, has redeemed us from death which, after the creation, had become our lot through Adam's fall and in which we would have perished eternally. Now think: just as in the first article you were to consider yourself one of God's creatures and not doubt it, now you must think of yourself as one of the redeemed and never doubt that. Emphasize one word above all others, the first word "our," as in Jesus Christ, "our" Lord. Likewise, suffered for "us," died for "us," arose for "us."[46] All this is ours and pertains to us; that "us" includes yourself, as the word of God declares.

Second, you must be sincerely grateful for such grace and rejoice in your salvation.

46. Luther repeatedly stressed that God is "for us," not "against us." The full significance of Christ becomes apparent only when a person realizes that Christ was given "for me" or "for us."

Man of Sorrows
by Albrecht Dürer, 1509

Third, you must sorrowfully lament and confess your shameful unbelief and mistrust of such grace. Oh, what thoughts will come to mind—the idolatry you have practiced repeatedly, how much you have made of praying to the saints and of innumerable works of yours which have opposed such salvation.

Fourth, pray now that God will preserve you from this time forward to the end in true and pure faith in Christ our Lord.

The Third Article of Sanctification[47]

"I believe in the Holy Spirit," etc. This is the third great light that teaches us where such a Creator and Redeemer may be found and outwardly encountered in this world, and what this will all come to in the end. Much could be said about this, but here is a summary: Where the holy Christian church exists, there we can find God the Creator, God the Redeemer, God the Holy Spirit, that is, the one who daily sanctifies us through the forgiveness of sins, etc. The church exists where the word of God concerning such faith is rightly preached. Again you have occasion here to ponder long about everything that the Holy Spirit accomplishes in the church every day, etc. Therefore be thankful that you have been called and have come into such a church. Confess and lament your lack of faith and gratitude, that you have neglected all this, and pray for a true and steadfast faith that will remain and endure until you come to that place where all endures forever, that is, beyond the resurrection from the dead, in life eternal. Amen.

47. Sanctification refers to the process of renewal that takes place in a person's life through the work of the Holy Spirit. Luther always made a careful distinction between justification and sanctification, though he also saw a cause-and-effect relationship between them. A sinner is justified or viewed with favor by God as a result of the imputation of Christ's righteousness. The righteousness that saves is an "alien and external righteousness," not a product of human efforts to live rightly. Faith in Christ alone makes sinners pleasing to God, but true faith also becomes active in love. In gratitude for the gift of forgiveness, a Christian will struggle against the continuing influence of sinful impulses and will perform good works for the sake of others. Luther attributes this reorientation of a person's life to the work of the Holy Spirit. In *The Small Catechism*, he says: "the Holy Spirit has called me through the gospel, enlightened me with his gifts, made me holy and kept me in true faith" (BC, 355). See also Martin Luther, *The Freedom of a Christian* (LW 31:327–77; TAL 1:467–538).

Image Credits

163, 168, 182, 183, 197, 254, 261, 272: Courtesy of the Richard C. Kessler Reformation Collection, Pitts Theological Library, Candler School of Theology, Emory University.

166, 266, 279: Wikimedia Commons.

158, 198–200: public domain / scanned from facsimile of 1529 printing of *Ein bet buclin / mit eym Calender und Passional/ hubsch zu gericht Martin. Luther.* Wittenberg.

161: Courtesy Houghton Library, Harvard University.

162: Wikimedia Commons / Web Gallery of Art.

175: Wikimedia Commons / Rijksmuseum Amsterdam online catalogue.

179, 265: Wikimedia Commons / The Yorck Project.

193: Wikimedia Commons / www.culture.pl.

256: Wikimedia Commons / www.geheugenvannederland.nl.

257: Wikimedia Commons / user: Urban.

259: Wikimedia Commons / gwGj6BUX8D5Kug at Google Cultural Institute.

271: Wikimedia Commons / National Gallery of Art: online database: entry 1941.1.20.

280: Wikimedia Commons / FQHhearPcv2ltw at Google Cultural Institute.